I0124342

Road
to
Recovery

The **Institute of Southeast Asian Studies (ISEAS)** was established as an autonomous organization in 1968. It is a regional centre dedicated to the study of socio-political, security and economic trends and developments in Southeast Asia and its wider geostrategic and economic environment. The Institute's research programmes are the Regional Economic Studies (RES, including ASEAN and APEC), Regional Strategic and Political Studies (RSPS), and Regional Social and Cultural Studies (RSCS).

ISEAS Publishing, an established academic press, has issued more than 2,000 books and journals. It is the largest scholarly publisher of research about Southeast Asia from within the region. ISEAS Publishing works with many other academic and trade publishers and distributors to disseminate important research and analyses from and about Southeast Asia to the rest of the world.

Road
to
Recovery

Singapore's Journey through the Global Crisis

Sanchita Basu Das

ISEAS

INSTITUTE OF SOUTHEAST ASIAN STUDIES
Singapore

First published in Singapore in 2010 by ISEAS Publishing
Institute of Southeast Asian Studies
30 Heng Mui Keng Terrace
Pasir Panjang
Singapore 119614

E-mail: publish@iseas.edu.sg
Website: http://bookshop.iseas.edu.sg

All rights reserved. No part of this publication may be reproduced, stored in a retrieval system, or transmitted in any form or by any means, electronic, mechanical, photocopying, recording or otherwise, without the prior permission of the Institute of Southeast Asian Studies.

© 2010 Institute of Southeast Asian Studies, Singapore

The responsibility for facts and opinions in this publication rests exclusively with the author and her interpretations do not necessarily reflect the views or the policy of the publisher or its supporters.

ISEAS Library Cataloguing-in-Publication Data

Basu Das, Sanchita.
   Road to recovery : Singapore's journey through the global crisis.
   1.   Global Financial Crisis, 2008-2009.
   2.   Financial crises—Singapore.
   3.   Singapore—Economic conditions.
   4.   Singapore—Economic policy.
   5.   Monetary policy—Singapore.
   I.   Title.
   II.   Title: Singapore's journey through the global crisis
HB3814 D22   2010

ISBN 978-981-4311-05-2 (soft cover)
ISBN 978-981-4311-04-5 (E-Book PDF)

Typeset by International Typesetters Pte Ltd
Printed in Singapore by Utopia Press Pte Ltd

For my parents

Contents

List of Tables

List of Figures

List of Boxes

Foreword

When I received the manuscript of this book from Ms Sanchita Basu Das, Lead Researcher for Economic Affairs in the ASEAN Studies Centre at the Institute of Southeast Asian Studies, I was, for a brief moment, reminded of the thoughts that ran through my head when I first heard the news of the collapse of Lehman Brothers. I felt at that time that the world was witnessing the beginning of something that may be a lot worse than any of the crises we have been through in our working lives. But nothing prepared me for the quantum of loss that the world suffered, both in financial and human terms.

There have been a lot of books written subsequently on what happened during those tumultuous days, and on the coordinated response of governments in the subsequent months. However, I was happy to see that this particular manuscript focuses on the actions taken specifically by Singapore policymakers to manage the effects of the crisis. Singapore has over the past few decades transformed itself into a major financial centre, a contemporary global city that attracts talents internationally. Yet, being a city that bridges the East and West, Singapore was one of the first in Asia to bear the brunt of the global crisis in 2008.

This book gives an insight into both the global crisis and the experience of Singapore. Aptly titled *The Road to Recovery*, it has indeed been a journey for the residents of this country, who endured pain and misery in the immediate aftermath of the crisis, but then slowly marched towards a recovery, albeit a fragile one. The directions to this path were of course led by the Singapore Government, who enacted Singapore's most radical budget ever in 2009. At the same time the Monetary Authority of Singapore kept a close watch on the currency to ensure it did not go through the same wild fluctuations that befell the G-10 currencies. As a result, when the global economy showed signs of turning around in the second quarter of 2009, Singapore was one of the first countries to benefit. Indeed the spectacular quarter-on-quarter growth in Q3-2009 was as much a testimony to the global recovery as to the immediate effects of the policy changes.

Ms Basu Das, an alumnus of NUS Business School, has written an accessible and comprehensive study on the crisis. The book presents a balanced opinion and provides a clear economic perspective for the city state in the post-crisis global economy. In addition, it gives a bird's eye view of the road map to the future for Singapore, which will hopefully make the country a lot more self sufficient than it has been in the past. The book will be suitable for academics as well as students of economics and policy studies. It will also be useful for those who are curious to know what happened behind the scenes during the crisis in the circle of policymakers. I hope you will enjoy reading and learning from the book!

Professor Bernard Yeung
Dean and Stephen Riady Distinguished Professor of Finance
NUS Business School

Acknowledgements

Writing this book has been a wonderful and enriching experience for me, which would not have been possible without the help, support, and advice of my colleagues and family. The Institute of Southeast Asian Studies (ISEAS), Singapore provided me with the platform to write a book on Singapore and the global economic crisis. For this I am grateful to ISEAS Director Ambassador K. Kesavapany who gave me the original inspiration to set about writing this book. I would like to thank Lee Poh Onn, Regional Economic Studies Programme Coordinator at ISEAS, for his encouragement and timely advice. Many thanks go also to Ambassador Rodolfo C. Severino, Head of the ASEAN Studies Centre at ISEAS, for his support and cooperation in letting me write the book in addition to my core responsibility in the centre. My sincere thanks to Triena Ong, Managing Editor of ISEAS Publishing, and Stephen Logan, Editor – Special Projects, for guiding me through the publishing process.

I owe my sincere gratitude to Manu Bhaskaran, Partner/ Head of Economics Research, Centennial Group Holdings, for his valuable comments and advice on what I had got wrong or forgotten while writing the book. Thanks also go to Kee Rui Xiong, Economist at the Macroeconomic Surveillance Department of the Monetary Authority of Singapore, who read and gave feedback on sections of the draft manuscript. I am privileged to have the Foreword by Prof. Bernard Yeung, Dean of NUS Business School, which I earnestly acknowledge.

Writing this book was also a test for my family, and I am grateful for their support. I wish to thank my husband, Subhro, whose encouragement and understanding as well as his constructive comments were very important for the completion of this book. My son, Adi, gave me the break from work that made writing the book easier, and I thank him for that. I would also like to extend my appreciation to my in-laws, Amita and Subhrendu Das, for always reading my write-ups with interest. I truthfully thank my parents, Pratima and Sankar Nath Basu, who have always associated themselves to the fullest extent with all my work, both when I was a student and now when I am a professional. I dedicate this book to them.

Abbreviations

3mma	three-month moving average
ACU	Asian currency units
ADB	Asian Development Bank
AEC	ASEAN Economic Community
AIG	American Insurance Group
ASEAN	Association of Southeast Asian Nations
AWS	Annual Wage Supplement
BIS	Bank of International Settlements
BLP	Bridging Loan Programme
bn	billion
CAR	capital adequacy ratio
CET	continuing education and training
CMI	Chiang Mai Initiative
CMIM	Chiang Mai Initiative Multilateralization
CPF	Central Provident Fund
CPI	consumer price inflation
DBU	domestic banking units
ECB	European Central Bank
EDB	Economic Development Board
EIU	Economic Intelligence Unit
EME	emerging market economies
ESC	Economic Strategies Committee
EU	European Union
FDI	foreign direct investment
FGIP	Finance Graduate Immersion Programme
FTA	free trade agreement

FX	foreign exchange
FY	fiscal year (April–March)
G-20	Group of Twenty
G-3	United States, eurozone, and Japan
GDP	gross domestic product
GFSR	Global Financial Stability Report
GIC	Government Investment Corporation
GST	goods and services tax
H1-2008	first half of 2008
ILO	International Labour Organization
IMF	International Monetary Fund
IR	Integrated Resorts
IT	information technology
JCS	Job Credit Scheme
KLSE	Kuala Lumpur Stock Exchange
LIBOR	London Interbank Offered Rate
LHS	left hand side
MAS	Monetary Authority of Singapore
M&A	mergers and acquisitions
MEPS	MAS Electronic Payment System
MMA	month moving average
MNC	multinational corporation
MOF	Ministry of Finance
MOM	Ministry of Manpower
MRT	Mass Rapid Transit
MTI	Ministry of Trade and Industry
MVC	monthly variable component
NAFTA	North American Free Trade Agreement
NEER	nominal effective exchange rate
NII	net investment income
NODX	non-oil domestic exports

NPL	non-performing loans
NWC	National Wages Council
PIC	Productivity and Innovation Credit
PMETs	professionals, managers, executives, and technicians
Q1-2009	first quarter of 2009
q/q	quarter-on-quarter
R&D	research and development
RHS	right hand side
sa	seasonally adjusted
saar	seasonally adjusted annualized rate
SG$	Singapore Dollar
SIBOR	Singapore Interbank Offered Rate
SME	small and medium enterprises
SPUR	Skills Programme for Upgrading and Resilience
SRI	Special Risk-Sharing Initiative
STI	Straits Times Index
SWF	sovereign wealth fund
TARP	Troubled Assets Relief Programme
UEN	Unique Entity Number
UK	United Kingdom
U.S.	United States
US$	U.S. Dollar
WB	World Bank
WDA	Workforce Development Agency
WEO	*World Economic Outlook*
WIS	Workfare Income Supplement
YA	year of assessment
Y/Y	year-on-year

1
Introduction

From 2004 to the middle of 2007, the world economy was growing strongly, world trade was burgeoning, inflation was low, liquidity in capital markets was abundant, the financial sector was providing remarkable returns, profitability was high, and asset prices were rising.

Yet, there were a few things that were disregarded by economists and financial experts. First, the real estate prices were rising astronomically, particularly in the United States, and a growing securitization business[1] was facilitating a huge growth in credit. At the same time a major imbalance was surfacing. While one group of countries (Japan, China, and the oil-exporting countries) was saving too much, there were others like the United States, and Europe who were borrowing to finance consumption and investment. These developments were unsustainable and needed a very minor catalyst to cause havoc in the financial markets and the world economy.

In the end, it was the booming U.S. housing market which proved to be the nemesis. Low interest rates and abundant liquidity in the system encouraged banks and financial institutions, particularly in the United States, to lend to sub-prime borrowers. When the interest rates started to rise, a large proportion of borrowers began to default resulting in failure or huge losses by several large financial institutions. The U.S. crisis thereafter spread to other financial markets and spilled over to the real economy by end 2008, leading to recession in several economies across the globe.

Governments around the world were forced to act swiftly to avert the failure of their financial systems and arrest the decline of economic growth. Unprecedented steps in conducting monetary and fiscal policy were taken to fix the financial dislocation and the weakness in the economic system. Initially, central banks focused their attention on easing liquidity to alleviate tensions in the financial markets. They loosened the terms and availability of existing central bank facilities. Policy interest rates were cut by almost all countries. In addition to monetary policy, nations also dug into their fiscal policy measures. Being the epicentre of the crisis, the U.S. Government took the lead by sanctioning US$700 billion under the Troubled Assets Relief Programme (TARP) to strengthen the U.S. financial market. For most of the developing economies, the fiscal stimulus packages ranged from 2.0 per cent of 2008 gross domestic product (GDP) to a maximum of 8.0 per cent of 2008 GDP. The crisis also pushed forward initiatives at the regional levels. ASEAN (Association of Southeast Asian Nations) Plus Three[2] initiated the Chiang Mai Initiative Multilaterialization (CMIM) Agreement and created a useful US$120 billion currency swap and crisis management facility for regional economies.

Thus, as the crisis turned out to be more global in nature, policy responses became more coordinated, but remained informal. Policymakers across the world did almost the same thing at the same time and for the same reason.

All this set the stage for the global economy to expand again. The International Monetary Fund (IMF) has projected the global economy to grow by 3.9 per cent in 2010 and another 4.3 per cent in 2011. However, the pace of recovery across economies is expected to remain uneven and slow especially on concerns about willingness of governments to continue providing fiscal and monetary stimulus packages to their economies. Moreover, the key adjustments needed in the U.S. economy — Asia's largest market — are not happening very quickly and convincingly.

Many described the 2008 financial crisis as "unprecedented". This was mainly on account of:

1. The speed at which the events happened: In a space of just eighteen months starting middle of 2007, multiple events resulted in one of the greatest assaults on global economic stability. It was not simply a crisis for the world's largest private financial institutions, but a crisis for credit markets, property markets, and equity markets. By early 2009, global equity markets had lost approximately US$32 trillion in value since their peak, credit markets around the world had suffered acute squeeze, and housing prices plummeted in many countries.

2. The scale of the impact, which had become global: Though it started off as a financial crisis, it soon became a general economic crisis, which in turn led to an employment and social crisis. It was a crisis which was simultaneously individual, national, and global and affected both the developed and the developing countries in the world. According to

the IMF, the global real economy faced one of its toughest periods on record and advanced economies experienced contraction for the first time in sixty years. In developed countries, this caused the number of unemployed to rise by eight million. In developing countries, the International Labour Organization (ILO) predicted that the financial and economic crisis might push more than a hundred million people into poverty.

(3) The range of unconventional measures taken by policymakers globally to arrest the falling confidence and economic activities: The severe economic downturn that accompanied the financial crisis led to activation of counter-cyclical fiscal and monetary policy actions of unprecedented magnitudes. Initially, the fiscal measures focused on improving the balance sheet of the financial and corporate sectors as reflected in large-scale bailouts in the United States and other advanced economies. The emerging market economies (EMEs) also undertook various policy measures to limit the adverse impact of contagion. However, there was one distinguishing feature. While for the advanced countries the policy priorities were to restore normalcy and strengthen financial regulation and supervision, for the EMEs priorities lay with the reversal of capital flows and collapse of trade. Nevertheless, restoring growth was the core objective among both sets of countries.

In addition, another feature that made the 2008 crisis exceptional was the fact that while many of the past crises in recent years had their roots in developing and emerging countries, the 2008 global financial crisis had its roots firmly in the United States. The financial crises over the past few decades often resulted from abrupt reversals in capital flows and from loose domestic, monetary, and fiscal policies. But in 2008 it was the "shadow" banking system[3] in the United States that led to excessive leverage positions both by the households and the banks. This resulted in heightened risk aversion and dried up capacity to lend.

During the 2008 crisis the decoupling theory between advanced and developing economies stood totally invalidated. Even if developing countries did not have much direct exposure to stressed financial instruments or institutions, the indirect impact through the real sector was by no means trivial. This brings forward significant challenges that need to be addressed on time in future.

First, policymakers around the world must take decisive actions to stall the fallout from the financial system to the real economy. It is crucial to inject capital into distressed financial institutions and tackle banks' impaired assets so as to ensure fast resumption of financial sector activities. This is not only important for the viable business to keep moving but also rebuild confidence for sustained recovery.

Second, policymakers should not lose sight of the future. Although it is important to quickly tackle the current issue, it should not turn out to be a burden in future and, thus, an "exit" strategy must be laid out in a timely manner. For instance, monetary conditions have been eased to ensure sufficient liquidity during the crisis. However, if this policy is left in place for too long it will generate inflationary risk and may create another basis of crisis in the medium-term. Again, fiscal stimulus needs to be sustained until the recovery is on a firm footing. But at the same time governments need to commit to large reductions in deficits once the recovery is on a solid footing and must start addressing long-term fiscal challenges by advancing reforms to put public finances on a more sustainable path. This is essential to create significant room for a counter cyclical policy, which will be needed to respond to future shocks.

Third, policymakers in one country need to consider the global dimension of their response to the crisis and the impact on other economies. For instance, the bank deposit guarantee scheme that was first introduced in Ireland started a domino effect and made its way to Asian economies. Hence, to minimize uncertainty, exit strategies to unwind various stimulus measures introduced by governments to stem the fallout of the global slowdown need to be coordinated both in terms of nature and timing.

Singapore and the Crisis

Financial crises are not new to Singapore; it was just a decade earlier when the country witnessed the 1997–98 Asian crisis, with capital flight and dramatic asset deflation resulting from an initial decline in export growth and shifting investor expectations. The city state was adversely affected through several channels. First, Singapore's exports to the crisis-hit economies (Thailand, Malaysia, Indonesia, and the Philippines) were badly affected as a result of severely diminished regional demand. Its exports to third-country markets became less competitive against the affected economies. Second, Singapore's banks were weakened by their sizeable lending exposure to crisis-affected countries. Third, Singapore suffered losses when Malaysia imposed exchange rate controls and the Kuala Lumpur Stock Exchange (KLSE) imposed a new rule requiring all trading in Malaysian shares to be done on the KLSE. The stock market and the property market in Singapore were badly hit during the crisis. Lastly, the Singapore dollar also had some contagion effects. The Singapore dollar declined 18.3 per cent over the six-month period to January 1998. However, the other regional currencies depreciated much more during the same period.

Yet, Singapore withstood the financial storm of 1997–98 that attacked the region and even managed to maintain a relatively favourable economic performance. Its GDP growth fell from a robust 8.9 per cent in 1997 to a mere 0.3 per cent for 1998. While admittedly low, Singapore's growth in 1998 was among the highest in the region.

A relatively better economic performance during the 1997–98 crisis showed Singapore's strong macroeconomic fundamentals, sound macroeconomic policies, and a willingness to take timely and effective policy measures to counter the adverse effects of the crisis. Following the outbreak of the crisis in July 1997, the Monetary Authority of Singapore (MAS) took steps to ease its monetary policy to cushion the rapidly decelerating Singapore economy. Subsequently, as the crisis became prolonged, Singapore policymakers worked towards cost-cutting measures (wage-cuts, property tax rebates, rental and utilities rebates by government agencies) and other measures like strengthening the economic infrastructure to arrest the slide in the economy. At the same time, the policymakers went ahead with financial sector reforms and liberalization to ensure the country's long-run competitiveness in the global economy.

Likewise, during the 2008 global economic and financial crisis, the Singapore economy was not completely insulated, as the country has strong trade and financial linkages with the rest of the world. The economy had weakened over the course of 2008, with an escalation in financial market turmoil and a more severe deceleration in global economic activities. Soon after the start of the crisis, net portfolio flows to Singapore reversed and thus had a knock-on effect on the stock market, which nosedived to record levels. The country suffered severely because of its high dependence on external demand. But the fundamentals of the city state's financial system and economy remained intact. Banks were well-capitalized and had limited direct exposure to toxic assets. Reserves were sufficient and the current account position was healthy.

The severity of the crisis compelled the Singapore policymakers to respond quickly and aggressively. The MAS decided aptly to depreciate the Singapore dollar, and the government put in place a range of fiscal and other measures to support lending and to cushion the impact of the global crisis. The 2009 budget, presented in January 2009, was designed to help the population keep jobs and help keep corporate bankruptcies down. In addition, policy measures were also introduced to build capabilities in the economy and the financial sector for the upturn. These, along with improving external factors, helped the Singapore economy to recover from the recession. Export growth turned positive while growth in the services sector firmed up. Confidence levels also edged up, and this translated into gains in asset markets, especially in the real estate sector. The unemployment rate fell and almost returned to near full-employment levels. Nevertheless, risks, mainly in the form of growth in the advanced economies and monetary and fiscal policies, remain for the city state economy.

Looking ahead, while the Singapore economy is looking for an output expansion of 5.5 to 6.5 per cent in 2010–11, it would likely have to accept a lower rate of growth in the long-run (Table 1.1). This is mainly because in the post-crisis era, global growth will be lower with the cost of massive fiscal and monetary policy responses taken into account for the crisis. Financial and corporate restructuring will exert considerable downward pressure on economic activities. Demand from the United States and Europe, the two most important export markets for Singapore, is likely to be dampened by the need to rebuild savings.

Hence, it is an opportune time for Singapore to restructure its economy and maximize growth capacity. In order to remain globally and regionally competitive, the city state must look for qualitative growth driven by skills, innovation, and productivity and weed out inefficiency. It has to enhance the quality of human capital and education standards in the country. In particular, there is an urgent need for improving the system of higher education and training. Continued investment in human capital would automatically enhance labour productivity and long-term growth. The country also has to invest heavily in research and development (R&D) and build up on its local technological base.

TABLE 1.1
Long-Term Singapore Economic Growth Rate

	1990–1995	1996–2000	2001–2003	2004–2007	2008–2009	2010–2015
GDP (average growth rate, %)	8.9	6.4	1.8	8.2	–1.1	4.3

Source: International Monetary Fund (IMF), *World Economic Outlook* database.

Acknowledging this, the Singapore Government has already turned its focus to longer-term development strategies. The Economic Strategies Committee (ESC), formed in May 2009, came up with a slew of recommendations that spurred a process of restructuring in the country. It had formulated seven key strategies that were grouped under three major policy goals: boosting skills in every job, deepening corporate capabilities, and making Singapore a distinctive global city and an endearing home (Figure 1.1). The next step will be implementation, which will bring in

FIGURE 1.1
ESC Key Strategies

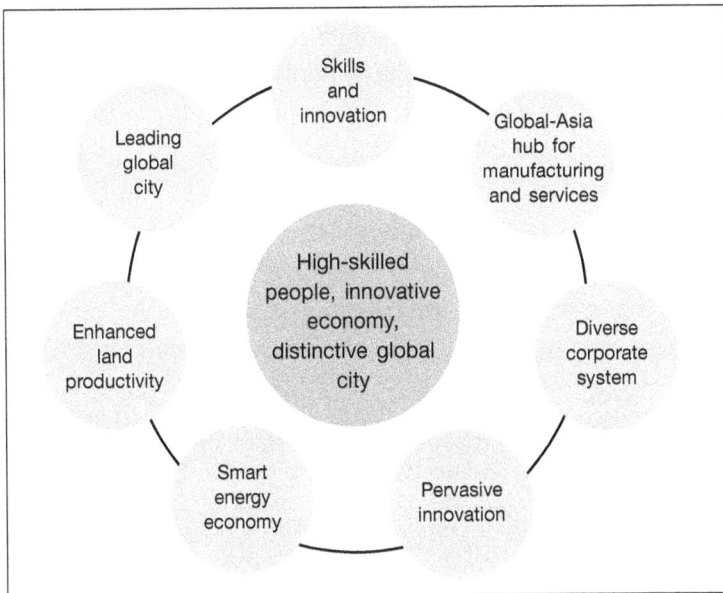

Skills and innovation

Leading global city

Global-Asia hub for manufacturing and services

High-skilled people, innovative economy, distinctive global city

Enhanced land productivity

Diverse corporate system

Smart energy economy

Pervasive innovation

Source: ESC Report.

further changes to the economy. However, the policymakers need to keep a few things in mind.

First, a few strategies suggested by ESC have already been tried before but they were later altered or discontinued as they were not able to completely meet the desired results. For example, there was a National Productivity Council, but it was transformed into SPRING Singapore and its role was also redefined to help small businesses. Again, the use of foreign-worker levies to control the inflow of foreign workers is not new. So to make these policies successful this time the government needs to provide the enabling environment. It must clearly define the ultimate goal of economic development and provide a framework for the development of the local corporate sector.

Second, an issue that needs careful consideration is that while the government will strongly support the implementation, businesses must also seek new ways to create value. They need to switch their focus from surviving the crisis to reacting to a post-crisis world where growth is expected to be slower and incremental demand is expected to come more from emerging market economies than in the past. Singapore companies need to undergo some restructuring in their operations to prosper in this new world.

Finally, to flesh out the ESC proposals on "phase shift" towards growth driven by skills, innovation, and focus on small and medium scale enterprises (SMEs), the FY2010 budget was also set on long-term, supply-side economic fundamentals. It did so by employing fiscal tools to promote economic growth driven more by productivity and innovation, nurture a more dynamic corporate sector, and ensure that economic growth remains inclusive in nature, so that all segments of Singapore's population benefit. However, all these initiatives only marked a starting point. Policymakers have to think of further changes if the goals of higher productivity growth and more inclusive growth are to be achieved in future.

About the Book

This book is essentially about the impact of the global economic crisis on Singapore and the policy responses by the Government of Singapore and the MAS. It also looks beyond the global crisis and gives an account of the government's initiatives to move into a knowledge-intensive era of economic development.

The next chapter (Chapter 2) gives an overview of the global financial and economic crisis so as to provide the background to what happened over the last few years. It first gives a short account of the genesis of the crisis, followed by the impact and the global policy response. Chapter 3 analyses the impact of the global economic crisis on the Singapore economy. It explores how an escalation of the financial crisis in September 2008 had provoked an unprecedented contraction of manufacturing activities and trade. This is followed by an examination of the Singapore Government's and Central Bank's policy responses to contain the knock-on effects of the crisis (Chapter 4). The fiscal policy discussed in the chapter mainly focuses on the 2009 budget as presented to the Parliament on 22 January 2009 (Table 4.1 shows the estimated figures). The budget figures changed during the course of 2009, and these numbers are discussed later in the chapter (Table 4.2). Chapter 5 discusses the economic projections over the medium-term and illustrates the required policies to promote a quality economic growth. The chapter looks beyond the global crisis, considering factors that will shape the landscape of the Singapore economy over the medium term. The last chapter (Chapter 6) wraps up the book with a summary of the lessons learnt from the crisis.

The global crisis started in August 2007 in the U.S. housing market. But it was the collapse of Lehman Brothers on 15 September 2008 that sent shock waves through the global financial system and got governments of the world to act overnight. Thereafter the financial crisis turned into an economic crisis as the advanced economies entered into a phase of recession. To avoid repetition, the crisis is referred to as "2008 crisis" in many places in the book.

Growth rates are an important mathematical tool to evaluate economic progress. All growth rates mentioned in the book are year-on-year (y/y) figures unless otherwise specified.

The book has used figures and charts extensively to show the impact of the crisis and the policy response thereafter. However, to keep it non-repetitive, all three periods are shown in any one graph: pre-crisis, during the crisis, post-crisis.

As economic events are unfolding every day, one can go on writing and never finish. That is why the cut-off date is set at 28 February 2010. What happened before that date is included, subsequent events are not.

The book is based on the information provided by publications on the subject by the World Bank (WB), the

International Monetary Fund (IMF), the Asian Development Bank (ADB), the Ministry of Finance, Ministry of Trade and Industry (MTI), Government of Singapore, the MAS, and the Economic Development Board (EDB). Use of material from these sources is gratefully acknowledged.

Notes

1. Securitization is a structured finance process that distributes risk by aggregating debt instruments in a pool, then issues new securities backed by the pool. To understand this simply, it is a method of financing assets. Rather than selling those assets "whole", the assets are combined into a pool, and then that pool is split into shares. Those shares are sold to investors who share the risk and reward of the performance of those assets.

2. ASEAN Plus Three comprises ten ASEAN countries (Brunei, Cambodia, Indonesia, Laos, Malaysia, Myanmar, the Philippines, Singapore, Thailand, and Vietnam) and China, Japan, and Korea.

3. This involves institutions (like Bear Stearns and Lehman Brothers) that are intermediaries between investors and borrowers. For example, an institutional investor like a pension fund may be willing to lend money, while a corporation may be searching for funds to borrow. The shadow banking system will channel funds from the investor(s) to the corporation, profiting either from fees or from the difference in interest rates between what it pays the investor(s) and what it receives from the borrower. Shadow institutions do not accept deposits and therefore are not subject to the same regulations as banks.

2
Global Financial and Economic Crisis: Causes, Impact, and Policy Response

The global financial turmoil surfaced in the middle of 2007 as a result of defaults of sub-prime mortgage loans in the United States. It was blown into an unprecedented financial crisis in 2008 when a series of major financial institutions in the United States and Europe started to fail. Around the world stock markets fell, financial institutions were bought out, and massive coordinated actions by the authorities were taken to inject liquidity into money markets and restore confidence in the financial systems. Strong calls were made at the Group of Twenty (G-20)[1] level for a new financial system to prevent future financial crises and to maintain global financial stability.

As the U.S. sub-prime mortgage crisis spread to the rest of the U.S. financial system and other industrialized-country financial markets, a significant slowdown was observed in economic growth of the U.S., Europe, and Japan. The financial sector crisis subsequently moved to the real economy. Although Asian financial institutions' exposure to sub-prime-related products was limited, the impact was felt through capital flow and trade channels.

Accordingly, the IMF in its *World Economic Outlook (WEO) Update* publication (January 2010) placed global growth at 3.0 per cent in 2008 and a contraction of –0.8 per cent in 2009. This represented a significant slide from an economic growth of 5.0 per cent observed in 2006–7. The advanced economies were in or close to recession in the second half of 2008 and early 2009, and showed some signs of recovery later in 2009. Growth in most emerging and developing economies was below trend, although key emerging economies in Asia, like China and India, showed higher resiliency.

Genesis of the Global Financial Crisis

The global financial crisis was triggered in August 2007 when the U.S. sub-prime loan defaults began to rise and foreclosures increased. At a fundamental level, however, the crisis could be attributable to the persistence of large global imbalances, which in turn was a result of a long period of loose monetary policy in the U.S. economy. This policy led to a prolonged period of abundant liquidity, imprudent lending in the sub-prime sector, lack of adequate regulation over financial institutions, and finally the collapse of the housing price bubble.

Following the demise of the dot-com bubble and the 9/11 terrorist attacks in 2001, monetary policy in the U.S. was eased aggressively. The target federal funds rate dropped from 6.5 per cent in January 2001 to 1.25 per cent two years later and stayed around that level until 2005 (Figure 2.1). Thereafter, the withdrawal of monetary accommodation was also quite gradual.

FIGURE 2.1
Federal Funds Target Rate in the U.S.

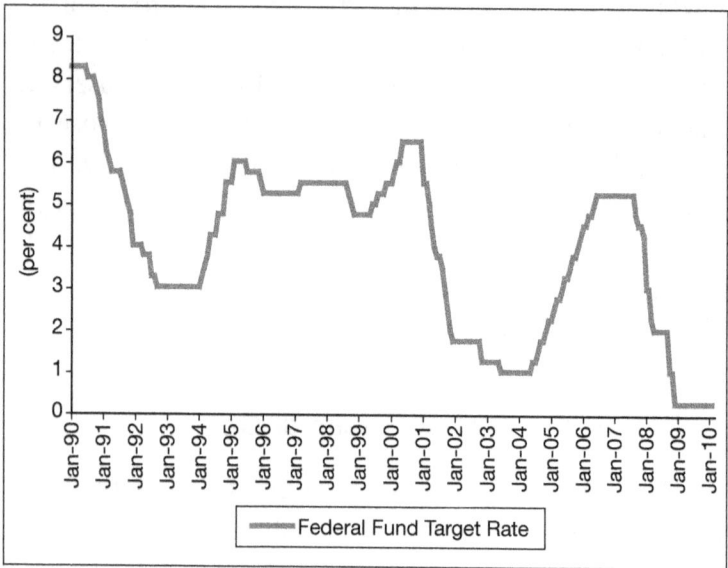

Source: Bloomberg.

This boosted consumption and investment in the United States as desired by the U.S. policymakers. Asset prices, particularly in housing and real estate, recorded strong gains providing further impetus to consumption and investment through wealth effects. Thus, aggregate demand in the United States consistently surpassed domestic output and this was reflected in large and growing current account deficits in the United States over the period (Table 2.1). The large domestic demand of the United States was met by the rest of the world, especially China and other East Asian economies, leading to growing surpluses in these

TABLE 2.1

Current Account Balance of Selected Economies (% of GDP)

Country	1990–94	1995–99	2000–04	2005	2006	2007	2008	2009
China	1.4	1.9	2.4	7.2	9.5	11.0	9.8	7.8
France	0.0	2.0	1.3	-0.6	-0.6	-1.0	-2.3	-1.2
Germany	-0.4	-0.8	1.4	5.1	6.1	7.5	6.4	2.9
India	-1.3	-1.3	0.5	-1.3	-1.1	-1.0	-2.2	-2.2
Japan	2.4	2.3	2.9	3.6	3.9	4.8	3.2	1.9
Korea	-1.0	1.9	2.1	1.8	0.6	0.6	-0.7	3.4
Malaysia	-5.2	1.8	9.8	15.0	16.7	15.4	17.9	13.4
Philippines	-4.0	-2.8	-0.7	2.0	4.5	4.9	2.5	3.2
Russia	0.9	3.5	11.2	11.0	9.5	5.9	6.1	3.6
Saudi Arabia	-11.7	-2.4	10.6	28.7	27.9	25.1	28.6	4.1
South Africa	1.2	-1.3	-0.7	-4.0	-6.3	-7.3	-7.4	-4.9
Switzerland	5.7	8.8	10.8	13.6	14.4	9.9	2.4	6.1
Thailand	-6.4	1.0	4.2	-4.3	1.1	5.7	-0.1	4.8
Turkey	-0.9	-0.8	-1.6	-4.6	-6.0	-5.8	-5.6	-1.8
United Arab Emirates	8.3	4.6	9.9	18.0	22.6	16.1	15.7	-1.6
United Kingdom	-2.1	-1.0	-2.0	-2.6	-3.4	-2.9	-1.7	-2.0
United States	-1.0	-2.1	-4.5	-5.9	-6.0	-5.3	-4.9	-2.6
Country Groups								
European Union	-0.6	0.5	-0.1	-0.1	-0.3	-0.5	-1.1	-0.8
ASEAN-5	-4.1	0.0	3.9	2.0	4.8	4.9	2.6	3.4
Middle East	-5.1	1.0	8.4	19.3	20.1	18.1	18.3	2.6

Note: "—" indicates deficit; 2009 figures are estimates.
Source: *World Economic Outlook* database, October 2009, IMF.

countries. These surpluses were again recycled to the
U.S. economy through purchase of U.S. Treasuries, thus
adding more fuel to the credit boom in the United States.
Meanwhile, the availability of relatively cheaper goods and
services from China and other emerging market economies
(EMEs) helped to maintain low inflation in the United
States, contributing to the persistence of accommodative
monetary policy.

Apart from creating large global imbalances, the
existence of very low interest rates for an extended period
of time encouraged the search for yield globally, which was
reflected in record high volume of capital flows (Figure 2.2)

FIGURE 2.2

Capital Flows to Emerging Market Economies

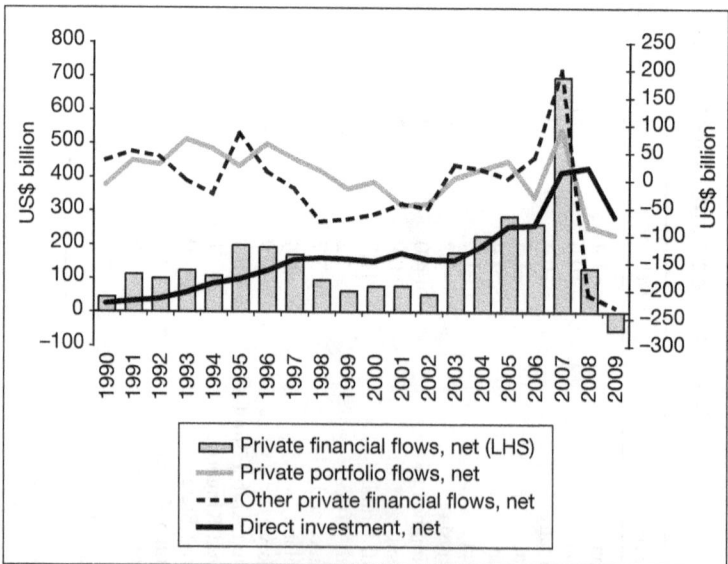

Source: *World Economic Outlook* database, October 2009, IMP.

to the EMEs. This was supported by financial institutions who, instead of just providing money through mortgage loans and collecting interest and repayments, further repackaged the loans into complex structured products. These were then sold to investors. During this time, due to macroeconomic stability, lending standards were relaxed and risks were underpriced. While this was regarded with suspicion by several central banks from time-to-time, it was felt that these risks were widely dispersed through financial innovation and that they would not pose a threat to the financial system.

Moreover, the five years through 2007 also saw a range of perverse incentives in financial markets: too much compensation for short-term returns, and not enough downside for losses perpetrated by the individuals receiving that compensation. Many of them were given attractive financial incentives for taking risks with the capital of the institutions of which they were a part. The risks they took essentially resulted in positive returns most of the time, but they came with a small probability of disaster. But, it was understood that if a disaster struck, it would result in losses to the financial institutions that had put their capital at risk, and a loss of confidence in the wider financial system. Nevertheless, the credit rating agencies seemed to encourage these activities by giving high ratings to products put forward by investment banks.

The combined effect of these developments was a large rise in mortgage credit to households, particularly those with a marginal credit quality. Most of these loans were with low margin money and with small teaser payments in the initial years. All this led to a boom in asset prices

(Figure 2.3) and excessive leverage of entities in financial markets.

As long as housing prices were rising, creditors felt safe in lending on appreciating collateral, which in turn contributed to further housing demand and prices. However, as inflation started to creep up in early 2004, the U.S. Federal Reserve started to withdraw monetary accommodation. With interest rates beginning to edge up, mortgage payments also started to rise. Tight monetary policy contained aggregate demand, thus lowering housing prices.

Once housing prices started to fall in 2006, sub-prime defaults began to rise and spread even to prime loans and

FIGURE 2.3
U.S. and European House Price Inflation

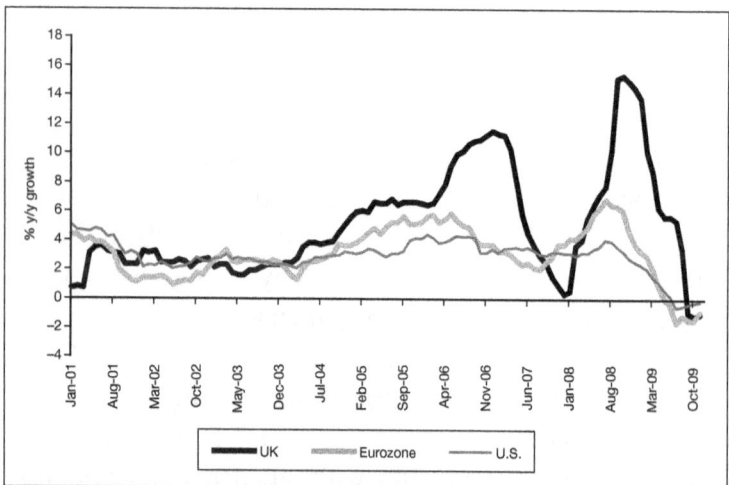

Source: Bloomberg, author's calculation.

other consumer credit. By early 2007, the first tremors of the crisis were felt as financial institutions stopped making new loans. This was based on the realization of the high risk associated with giving mortgages to people with poor credit records. At the same time, rising interest rates led to a rapid rise in defaults by mortgagees who could not handle the larger installments compared to the low interest years. The crisis deteriorated further in mid-2007, when foreclosures of U.S. homes went up by 93 per cent from a year earlier. Alarm bells rang on Wall Street as a number of banks and financial institutions started revealing major positions in the mortgage markets, which they were unable to get rid of due to a lack of liquidity in these instruments. The first quarter of 2008 saw the demise of Bear Stearns and a contagion effect into European and United Kingdom markets. But nothing had quite prepared the world for the fury of September, which started with the seizure of Fannie Mae and Freddie Mac by the U.S. Government, but ultimately ended with the bankruptcy of Lehman Brothers, the swallowing of Merrill Lynch by Bank of America, and a massive injection of capital into American Insurance Group (AIG). Liquidity disappeared for even the most basic of interbank lending instruments, and the world was staring at a crisis that had many parallels with the Great Depression in the United States in the 1930s (Box 2.1).

Given the growing financial globalization, soon banks and financial institutions in other major advanced economies, especially Europe, were also adversely affected by losses and capital write-offs (Figure 2.4). Government bailouts were announced for major banks in Europe. Many

BOX 2.1
Chronology of Major Events

The crisis in world financial markets began when prices started declining in the U.S. real estate market in late 2006.

March/April 2007: New Century Financial corporation stops making new loans. The IMF warns of risks to global financial markets from weakened U.S. home mortgage market.

July/August 2007: German banks, including IKB Deutsche Industriebank, Saxony State Bank, and Bavaria State Bank, are caught up in the crisis. U.S. President George W. Bush rejects government intervention. He later pledges help for struggling homeowners to help ease the mortgage crisis.

September 2007: British bank Northern Rock is besieged by worried savers; the bank is nationalized. The U.S. Federal Reserve starts a series of interest rate drops.

October 2007: Profits at Citigroup drop sharply. The IMF lowers 2008 growth forecast.

January 2008: Swiss bank, UBS, reports more than US$18 billion in writedowns. In the United States, Bank of America acquires Countrywide Financial. The Federal Reserve slashes the interest rate to 3 per cent.

February 2008: Fannie Mae, the largest source of money for U.S. home loans, reports a US$3.55 billion loss for the fourth quarter of 2007, three times what had been expected.

March 2008: Bear Stearns is forced to accept a buyout by JP Morgan Chase. The deal is backed by Federal Reserve loans of US$30 billion.

In Germany, Deutsche Bank reports a loss of 141 million euros for the first quarter of 2008. The Federal Reserve spearheads coordinated actions by world central banks.

Carlyle Capital defaults on US$16.6 billion of indebtedness. The United States frees up another US$200 billion to back troubled Fannie Mae and Freddie Mac.

July 2008: California mortgage lender IndyMac collapses. Spain's largest property developer, Martinsa-Fadesa, declares insolvency.

7 September: U.S. Government seizes control of Fannie, Freddie in US$200 billion bailout.

15 September: Lehman Brothers investment bank declares US$600 billion bankruptcy. Merrill Lynch acquired by Bank of America.

17 September: United States bails out AIG insurance giant for US$85 billion.

19 September: White House requests US$700 billion bailout plan from Congress.

22 September: Morgan Stanley and Goldman Sachs convert to bank holding companies.

26 September: Federal Reserve seizes Washington Mutual in largest-ever U.S. bank failure.

29 September: Governmental bail-outs announced for key banks in Britain and Germany; state takeover of a bank in Iceland. British Government intervenes to save major mortgage lender Bradford & Bingley. Netherlands, Belgium, and Luxembourg to take over substantial parts of Fortis. German Finance Ministry announces that government and top banks were moving to inject billions of euros into troubled mortgage lender Hypo Real Estate.

30 September: Wachovia Bank starts negotiating with Citigroup for takeover deal.

1 October: U.S. Senate adopts massive bail-out plan.

3 October: Wells Fargo Bank and Wachovia Corp announce
merger.

Source: Adapted from Deutsche Welle DW-World.de, "Chronology: Financial
Crisis Spreads From US to World Markets", 4 October 2008 <http://www.
dw-world.de/dw/article/0,,3689713,00.html>.

moved to guarantee all private savings accounts in the
countries to reassure depositors and stop the panic.

As a result, transactions in global interbank markets
began to freeze on the perceived rise in counterparty
risks, exacerbating the liquidity problem even for healthier

FIGURE 2.4
Estimates of Global Bank Write-downs, 2007–10

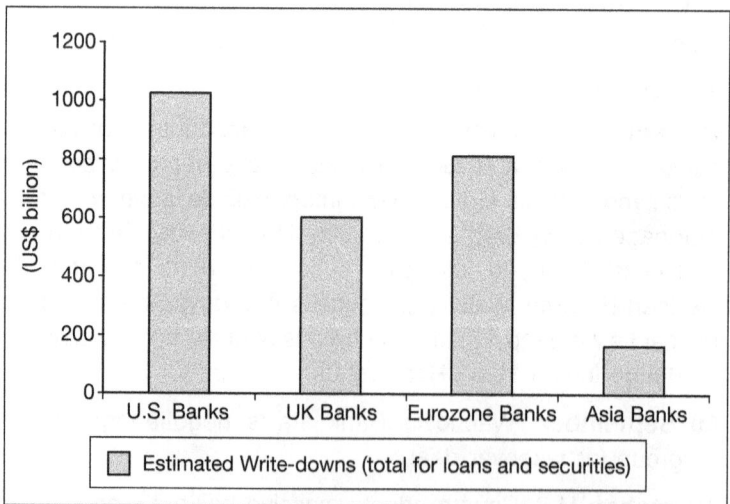

Source: IMF *Global Financial Stability Report,* October 2009.

financial institutions. The London Interbank Offered Rate (LIBOR) shot up, with the differential between the overnight LIBOR and the federal funds rate spiking to over 300–400 basis points in October 2008 (Figure 2.5). There was a wholesale flight of capital to safety, which has been reflected in large capital outflows from the EMEs and very low yields on Treasury bills and bonds (Figure 2.6). These developments were significantly accentuated following the default by Lehman Brothers and the rescue of AIG, thus resulting in a complete loss of confidence in the global financial system.

FIGURE 2.5
Three Months USD Interbank Rate

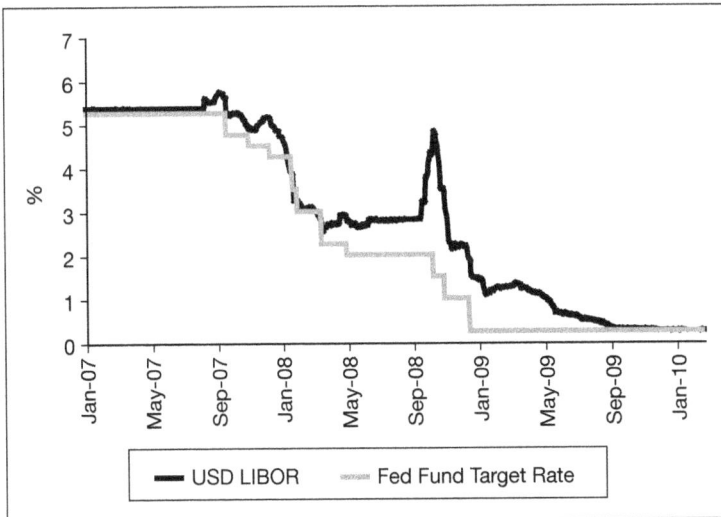

Source: Bloomberg.

FIGURE 2.6
Selected U.S. Interest Rates

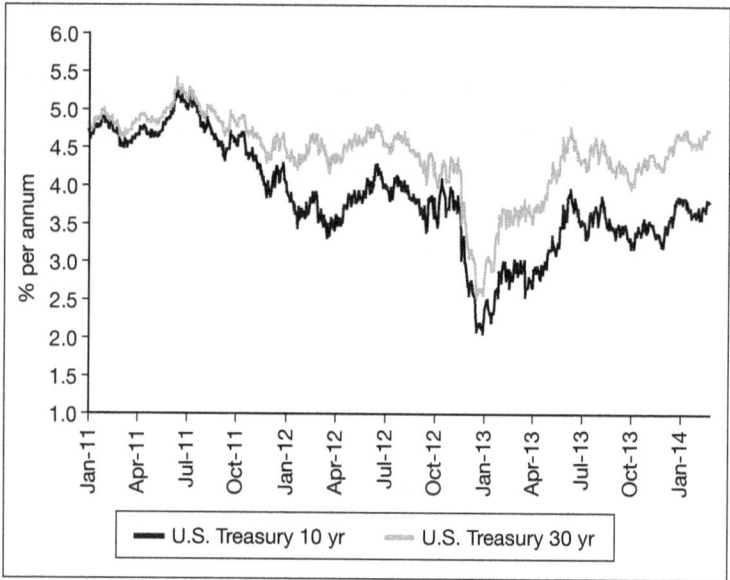

Source: Bloomberg.

Impact of the Crisis

The crisis in global financial markets in conjunction with
the sharp correction in a range of asset prices suddenly
led to a sharp contraction in economic activity. With
weak credit markets and significantly reduced consumer
spending, global trade shrank and industrial production fell
resulting in a synchronized economic downturn experienced
by both advanced as well as emerging and developing
economies. According to the IMF, world output contracted

by an alarming 6.25 per cent in the fourth quarter of 2008 (compared to a growth of 4.0 per cent growth a year earlier) and fell almost as fast in the first quarter of 2009. Both advanced and emerging economies experienced 7.5 per cent and 4.0 per cent decline respectively in real GDP during the fourth quarter of 2008.

The U.S. GDP growth turned negative in Q4-2008 and deepened further in the first two quarters of 2009 as personal consumption contracted on households' decreasing demand for durable goods. The deterioration in business sentiment drove firms to cut investment and employment. The cumulative job losses in the United States reached 3.1 million in 2008. The eurozone economies also contracted sharply in the fourth quarter of 2008 and later in early 2009, the drop being led by falling exports. Domestic demand also softened as the eurozone unemployment rate rose from 7.2 per cent at the start of 2008 to 8.5 per cent in February 2009. The Japanese economy also suffered from the economic slowdown; manufacturing production fell by 38 per cent in February 2009 and merchandise exports contracted by 41 per cent in Q1-2009 (Table 2.2).

In Asia (other than Japan), growth fell sharply in Q4-2008, led by a collapse in global trade (Figure 2.7). Within the region, growth has held up better in the larger, less trade dependent economies like China and India. However, the more export-dependent economies, such as Malaysia, Singapore, and Thailand, saw more pronounced declines, posting decelerating or negative growth as global demand for electronics and other goods tumbled. In addition, funding stresses arising from the financial turmoil

TABLE 2.2
GDP Growth Rates during the Crisis

(in y/y %)	2007	2008	Q3-2008	Q4-2008	Q1-2009	Q2-2009
United States	2.0	0.4	0.7	–0.8	–3.3	–3.8
Eurozone	2.7	0.6	0.6	–1.4	–4.9	–4.8
Japan	2.4	–0.7	–0.2	–4.3	–8.7	–7.2
Hong Kong	6.4	2.4	1.7	–2.5	–7.8	–3.8
Korea	5.1	2.2	3.1	–3.4	–4.2	–2.2
Taiwan	5.7	0.1	–1.0	–8.4	–10.1	–7.5
Singapore	7.9	1.0	0.04	–4.3	–9.5	–3.5
Indonesia	6.3	6.1	6.4	5.2	4.4	4.0
Malaysia	6.3	4.6	4.7	0.1	–6.2	–3.9
Thailand	4.9	2.6	3.9	–4.3	–7.1	–4.9
Philippines	7.2	3.8	5.0	4.5	0.6	1.5
China	13.0	9.0	9.0	6.8	6.1	7.9
India	9.2	7.5	7.6	5.3	5.8	6.1

Source: CEIC database, author's calculation.

FIGURE 2.7
Global Trade Volumes of Goods and Services

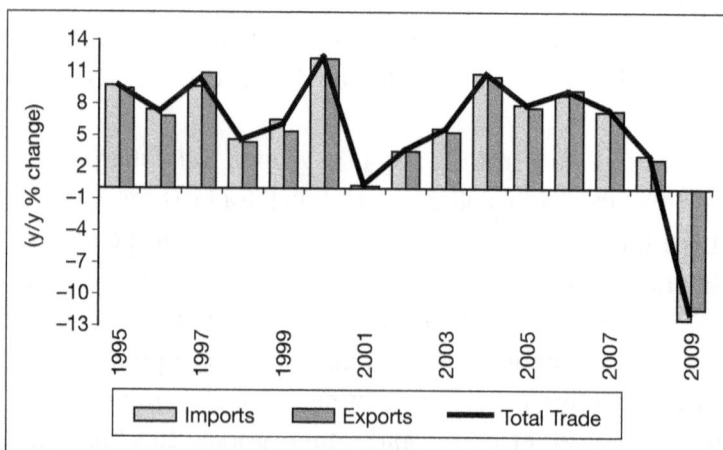

Source: *World Economic Outlook*, IMF, October 2009.

in the United States and Europe led to sharp reductions in investment spending across most parts of Asia.

In tandem with the rapid cooling of global activity, inflation pressures subsided quickly in the second half of 2008. Oil prices fell sharply from 2008 mid-year highs of US$145 per barrel to US$40 per barrel by the end of 2008 on weakening prospects for the emerging economies that have provided the bulk of demand growth in the recent past. At the same time, rising economic slack contained wage increases and eroded profit margins. As a result, headline inflation in the advanced economies declined towards the end of 2008 and finally fell below the 1 per cent mark in 2009 (Figure 2.8). Inflation has also moderated

FIGURE 2.8

Headline Inflation of Selected Regions
(average of the year)

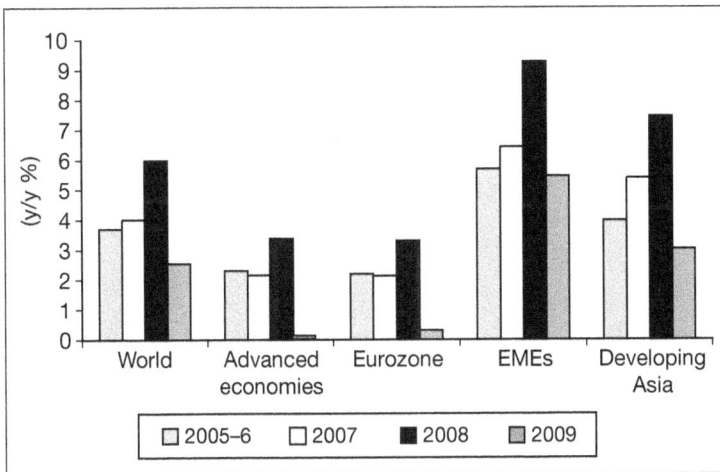

Source: *World Economic Outlook*, IMF, October 2009.

significantly across the emerging economies, especially in Asia, excluding Japan, where inflation fell from a peak of 7.1 per cent in June 2008 to 0.9 per cent in March 2009. While this helped the low-income consumers, it punished the oil-exporting countries like Indonesia, Thailand, Vietnam, and Malaysia both in terms of exports and government revenues.

Other than these, the economic crisis also had a profound impact on capital flows in developing countries, including Asia. Private capital inflows (net) to the EMEs fell from the peak of US$696 billion in 2007 to US$129 billion in 2008 and are estimated to record net outflows of US$52 billion in 2009. The sharp decline in capital flows in 2009 was mainly on account of outflows under bank lending and portfolio flows. This in turn impinged on exchange rate movements and on asset prices (Table 2.3).

Lastly, the developing economies were also challenged by the decline in remittances. This plays key roles in capital formation and household survival strategies in most of the EMEs, including India, China, the Philippines, Bangladesh, and Pakistan — five of the top ten remittance recipients in the world. Due to the 2008 crisis, South Asia, where remittances grew by almost 27 per cent in 2008, experienced a fall of 4–7 per cent in 2009. Remittances from overseas Filipinos grew by only 6–9 per cent, compared with 10–14 per cent in 2008 (Figure 2.9).

Despite the damage to the real economy, the banking system in most of emerging Asia had not been particularly badly affected. There were several reasons for this: the relatively limited exposure of Asian banks to sub-prime financial products in the United States, the greater emphasis

TABLE 2.3

Stock Market Crash and Exchange Rate Changes of Selected Countries

	Stock Market (month-end)			Exchange Rate (vis-à-vis US$)		
	June 2008	*March 2009*	*Change (%)*	*June 2008*	*March 2009*	*Change (%)**
United States	11,350	7,608	-33.0	—	—	—
Eurozone	3,315	2,036	-38.6	1.57	1.32	-15.9
Japan	13,481	8,109	-39.8	106.21	98.96	-6.8
Hong Kong	22,102	13,576	-38.6	7.79	7.75	-0.6
Korea	1,674	1,206	-28.0	1,046.05	1,383.1	32.2
Taiwan	7,523	5,210	-30.7	30.35	33.91	11.7
Singapore	2,947	1,699	-42.3	1.35	1.52	12.0
Indonesia	2,349	1,434	-39.0	9,228	11,700	26.8
Malaysia	1,186	872	-26.5	3.26	3.64	11.7
Thailand	768	431	-43.9	33.44	35.5	6.2
Philippines	2,459	1,986	-19.3	44.95	48.32	7.5
China	2,736	2,373	-13.3	6.85	6.83	-0.3
India	13,461	9,708	-27.9	43.04	50.73	17.9

Note: "–" implies appreciation.
Source: Bloomberg, author's calculation.

FIGURE 2.9
Change in Remittance Inflows (%)

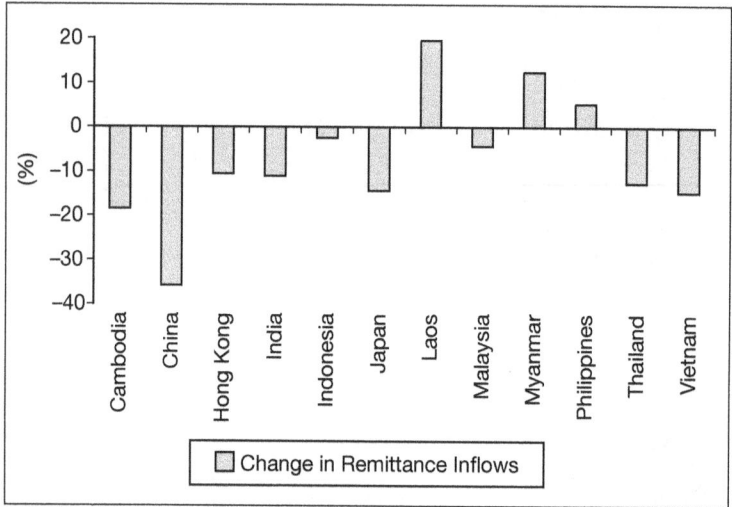

Notes: (i) Workers' remittances include migrant transfers. (ii) Comparison is
between 2008 and 2007 data; 2008 data are estimates.
Source: ADB.

on supervision and regulation in the banking systems of
the 1997–98 Asian crisis-affected economies (Thailand,
Malaysia, Korea), and the fact that several countries (China,
India, Vietnam) still have a significant part of the banking
system under public ownership and control.

Failure of the Decoupling Hypothesis and the Contagious Nature of the Crisis

Prior to the start of the crisis there was a lot of discussion
on the decoupling hypothesis. It was believed that even if
advanced economies go into recession, emerging economies

will remain unscathed because of their substantial foreign exchange reserves, improved policy framework, robust corporate balance sheet, and relatively healthy banking sector. However, in the face of the crisis, this was completely invalidated. This was mainly because in an increasingly globalized world no country would stand in isolation and any disturbance in a major country like the United States had to have a ripple effect on the rest of the world.

In this regard, the 2008 crisis was highly contagious in nature. The fallout of the crisis did not remain confined to the financial sector but also affected the real economy, pushing developed nations into deep recession. The economic crisis of this scale also affected other economies in the world. Most emerging market economies, with high export linkages, slowed down significantly. The blow also came from loss of investor confidence in financial systems and instruments. External financing, a key driver of economic expansion in the developing countries, was cut back radically. Declines or slower growth in remittances also damaged economies dependent on their overseas workers.

Singapore suffered a severe blow from the crisis. It was hit by a multiple transmission mechanism, which reiterated the failure of the decoupling theory. The city state went into recession in the first quarter of 2009 when the manufacturing exports dipped on downturn in the United States and other advanced markets.

World Response to the Crisis

The financial crisis led to emergency interventions in many national financial systems. As the crisis developed into a global recession, economic stimulus came into play as an important policy tool. Following the rescue plans for the banking system, major developed and emerging economies announced plans to relieve the stress of their financial systems. In particular, economic stimulus packages were announced in China, the United States, and the European Union. In the final quarter of 2008, the financial crisis saw the G-20 group of major economies assume a new significance as a focus of economic and financial crisis management.

Monetary and Fiscal Packages

As an immediate step to maintain confidence in financial markets, the monetary authorities acted quickly to adopt measures responding to the demand by financial institutions for increased access to central bank liquidity. Many gave guarantees for bank liabilities (like Singapore and Australia). The U.S. Federal Reserve authorized temporary foreign exchange swap lines with fourteen monetary authorities to alleviate the global shortage of dollar funding. In the Asia-Pacific, this included Singapore, Japan, and Korea. Measures were introduced to revive credit and capital flows. The U.S. Government sanctioned US$700 billion under the Troubled Assets Relief Programme (TARP)[2] to strengthen the U.S. banks and financial markets.

Subsequently, governments and central banks stepped in to assure relief to the stressed institutions and announced bailout packages to control the financial catastrophe. There were capital injections employed in many countries, but with different conditions attached depending on the jurisdiction and the circumstances of the institutions. There were programmes to deal with toxic assets by moving those assets off the balance sheets of institutions. Other types of actions included takeovers of financial institutions through substantial governmental control or forced mergers.

Besides injecting liquidity and introducing bailout packages, policy interest rates were cut by almost all countries and by end 2008 the policy action looked more coordinated. This was done to support domestic demand and to help the economies to ride out the economic slowdown. The U.S. Federal Reserve rate was reduced to a low of 0.25 per cent, while the European Central Bank (ECB) cut the key refinancing rate to 1.0 per cent and UK rates reached a low of 0.5 per cent. In the Asia-pacific, Bank Indonesia brought down its policy rate by 200 basis points from December 2008 to May 2009 to a low of 7.2 per cent. The Reserve Bank of Australia cut the benchmark lending rate by a record 4.25 percentage points to 3 per cent (a 49-year low) between September 2008 and April 2009 (Table 2.4). The MAS also undertook a slew of measures to address the issue of liquidity and drive up confidence. It maintained a higher level of Singapore dollar liquidity in the banking system and entered into a precautionary US$30 billion swap arrangement with the U.S. Federal Reserve. To restore confidence in the economy, the MAS abandoned its four-year-long strong Singapore dollar policy and shifted to zero appreciation.

Starting in late 2008, the discretionary fiscal policies were widely introduced to boost the domestic economy. Some were quite large, with the United States announcing a package of US$787 billion and China a package of US$585 billion. In Asia, Taipei, Korea, Malaysia, and Thailand

TABLE 2.4
Interest Rates in Selected Economies

Country	July 2008	December 2008	May 2009	Change in basis points (Dec 2008–May 2009)
United States	2.00	0–0.25	0–0.25	0
European Union	4.25	2.50	1.00	–150
United Kingdom	5.00	2.00	0.50	–150
Japan	0.50	0.10	0.10	0
Australia	7.25	4.25	3.00	–125
Singapore	1.00	1.00	0.69	–31
Indonesia	8.75	9.25	7.25	–200
Malaysia	3.70	3.37	2.13	–124
Thailand	3.50	2.75	1.25	–150
Hong Kong	2.30	0.95	0.31	–64
Korea	5.00	3.00	2.00	–100
China	4.14	2.79	2.79	0
India	6.00	5.00	3.25	–175

Source: UNDP, 2009.

announced packages of at least 4 per cent of 2008 GDP. Among the Pacific countries, Australia announced a fiscal stimulus package of 4.7 per cent of 2008 GDP and New Zealand, 4.3 per cent of 2008 GDP (Table 2.5).

It is difficult to conclude that the fiscal policy actions were coordinated, but they were all pointing in the same direction. In January 2009, Singapore announced a US$15 billion fiscal aid package, including tax breaks and assistance to help Singaporeans keep jobs and to help viable companies stay afloat.

TABLE 2.5

Fiscal Stimulus in Selected Countries/Economic Regions

Country Name	Amount, US$ bn
United States	1,487.0
European Union	254.6
Japan	225.0
Australia	29.0
Singapore	15.0
Indonesia	12.7
Malaysia	18.1
Thailand	45.3
Philippines	6.5
Vietnam	18.6
Korea	63.0
China	798.0
India	80.0

Note: Figures of some countries also include off-budget expenditures.
Source: UNESCAP and author's compilation from media sources.

G-20 Commitments

In April 2009, members of G-20 met to decide on concerted fiscal expansion amounting to US$5 trillion to resolve the crisis. They further agreed on over US$1 trillion of additional resources for the world economy through international financial institutions and trade finance. This was to ensure support for trade finance and to ensure availability of funds for the poor countries. The G-20 countries further pledged to implement tougher financial regulations, clamp down on tax havens, increase lending by multilateral development banks to assist developing countries, and avoid protectionist policies. They also agreed to put in place credible exit strategies to ensure long-term fiscal sustainability and price stability.

Chiang Mai Initiative

To build confidence in the Asian region, the Finance Ministers of ASEAN Plus Three decided to expedite the multilateralization of the Chiang Mai Initiative (CMI) and expand their commitments to a total of US$120 billion from US$90 billion earlier. The main objective of the pact was to address balance of payment and short-term liquidity difficulties in the region and to supplement the existing international financial arrangements. Of the total amount, China and Japan will contribute US$38.4 billion each to the liquidity pool and South Korea will offer US$19.2 billion. The ten ASEAN nations will together provide US$24 billion. They also plan to expand the local currency bond market as a source of investment and finance for the region.

Assessment of Policy Response

Policymakers around the world responded to the crisis in an unprecedented manner. This was mainly to prevent the global recession from turning into a prolonged depression. The fiscal and monetary policy measures were quite aggressive, and some measures were into uncharted territory. Most importantly, given the severity of the crisis, national responses were supplemented by global efforts. At the meeting of G-20 leaders, there were collective commitments on coordinated actions to revive growth, restore stability of financial systems, and rebuild confidence in financial markets and institutions.

All these measures taken by the governments and central banks seem to have had a favourable impact on the macro-economy and financial markets. Global activity was estimated to have risen by about 3.0 per cent during the second quarter of 2009, following a 6.5 per cent contraction in the first quarter of 2009. The nascent recovery was most evident in financial markets, as equity markets posted a strong gain (Figure 2.10) on return of confidence and rebound of international capital flows. While initially the main driver of economic recovery was public policy, improving growth prospects began to feed back into financial conditions, with declining risk aversion adding further momentum. For 2010, economists are expecting a gradual recovery, with the world economy posting a growth of 3.9 per cent.

However, the environment still remains challenging for lower-tier borrowers, notably small- and medium-size enterprises and many households (*Global Financial*

FIGURE 2.10
Major Equity Indices

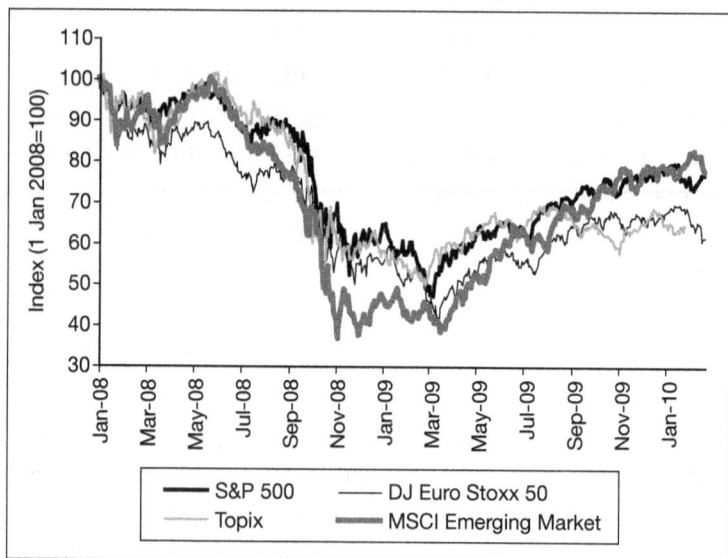

Source: Bloomberg, author's calculation.

Stability Report, October 2009, IMF). Securitization markets are still heavily impaired, which severely limits banks' capacity to disburse credit.

Summing Up

The sub-prime crisis that began in the U.S. housing market in 2007 snowballed into a global financial and economic crisis. The global financial landscape changed with failure of several large financial institutions and subsequent government intervention to prevent imminent collapse.

The lack of trust and uncertainty led to disruptions in the short-term funding markets and a fall in equity prices. The contagion of the crisis transmitted from the financial sector to the real sector through demand slump, production plunge, unemployment rise, and credit seize. Most worryingly, world trade — the main channel of crisis transmission — fell sharply. GDP growth rates fell for both advanced and developing economies, leading to contraction in global GDP for the first time since World War II.

The crisis had prompted countries around the world to come up with aggressive and unconventional monetary and fiscal policy measures. There were several instances of coordinated policy actions by the central banks. This averted an escalation of the crisis and prevented a meltdown of financial systems. Since the second quarter of 2009, the world economy has entered a phase of recovery, although the pace will probably remain sluggish for some time to come.

Notes

1. G-20 is a group of Finance Ministers and Central Bank Governors from twenty economies: Nineteen countries plus the EU. The G-20 is a forum for cooperation and consultation on matters pertaining to the international financial system.
2. The TARP is a programme of the U.S. Government to purchase troubled assets (i.e. illiquid and difficult-to-value assets) from banks and other financial institutions to strengthen its financial sector.

3
Impact of Global Economic Crisis on Singapore

After the onset of the global economic crisis in 2008, Singapore had become the first East Asian nation to fall into recession. The year-on-year growth rate had plunged from 7.7 per cent in 2007 to 4.5 per cent in H1-2008 (first half of 2008) and further to −9.5 per cent in Q1-2009 (first quarter of 2009). Although the exposure of Singapore's banks to sub-prime mortgage-linked securities was limited, the recession came mainly through the fall in non-oil exports. This is especially because Singapore has maintained an outward-looking policy over the past decade and has reduced barriers to international trade and investment. Its total trade to GDP ratio of close to 300 per cent is among the highest in the world, thus raising the economy's vulnerability to global economic shocks.

Transmission of Global Crisis to Singapore

There were at least three ways that the global developments were transmitted to the Singapore economy. While the financial sector was affected by the cessation of credit flows, the real economy suffered as the external demand for manufactured goods choked up. In addition, it was the working class that suffered from the worst consequences of the economic recession.

Impact on the Real Sector

Singapore's economy took a severe pounding from global financial sector turmoil and growth slowdown as the country's GDP shrank by an alarming rate of 15.2 per cent and 7.1 per cent quarter-on-quarter (q/q) seasonally adjusted annualized rate (saar) in Q4-2008 and Q1-2009 respectively. Year-on-year, the growth rate fell for three consecutive periods before hitting a low of –9.5 per cent in Q1-2009 (Figure 3.1).

FIGURE 3.1
Singapore GDP Growth Rate Fell Sharply

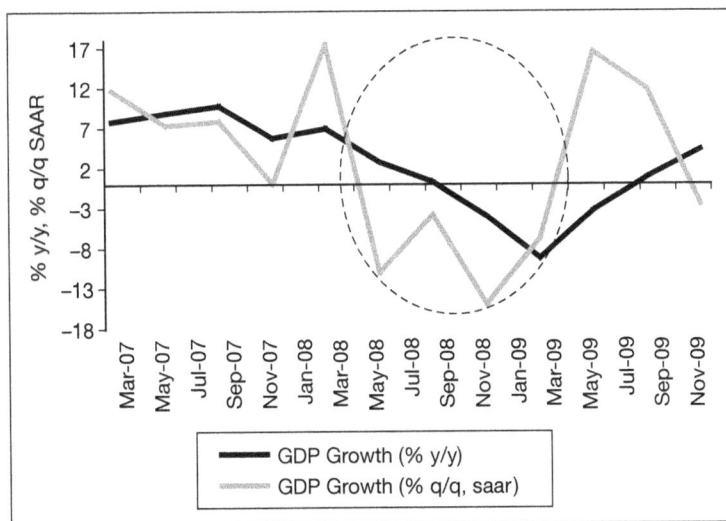

Source: CEIC Database, author's calculation.

This striking weakness in the Singapore real economy had been largely due to a marked contraction in the manufacturing sector (Figure 3.2). Production was badly depressed on the back of falling global export demand. The two key export destinations, the United States and Europe, grappling with the financial turmoil, still account for more than 33 per cent of the total non-oil exports (Table 3.1). Exports to ASEAN for domestic consumption were badly hit by declining purchasing power. Another factor that contributed to the fall in exports was the nature of cross-border production and trade flows that have developed in the region, particularly in the electronics industry. The fall in end-use demand from

FIGURE 3.2
Contraction in Manufacturing Sector

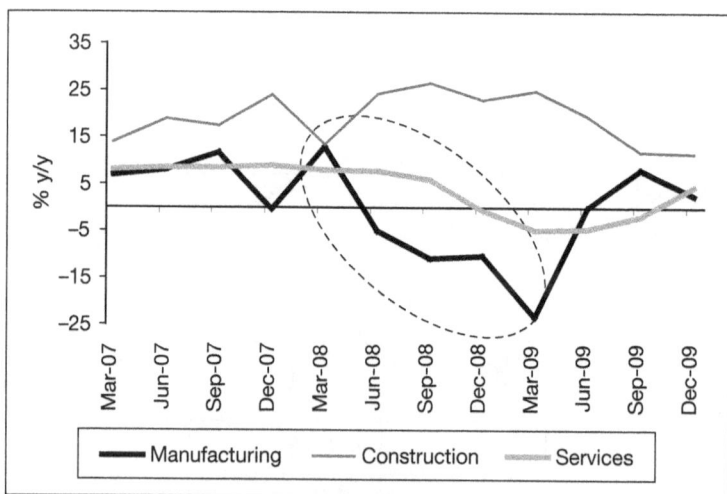

Source: CEIC Database, author's calculation.

TABLE 3.1

Market-share of Singapore's Total Non-oil Exports

	USA	Europe	Japan	Indonesia	Malaysia	Thailand	Hong Kong	Taiwan	China
2007 Share (% of total)	15.2	18.2	6.2	6.4	9.3	4.8	6.8	3.9	9.5

Source: *Yearbook of Statistics*, 2009, Singapore Department of Statistics.

the G-3 economies (United States, eurozone, and Japan) resulted in synchronized decline in intermediate goods exports across Asian economies. Moreover, the decline in intra-Asian trade flows was amplified as intermediate goods crossed national borders several times during the production process.

Trade financing constraints also affected trade flows in the last quarter of 2008, although the problem was eased quickly. Lastly, Singapore's exports also suffered due to price effect. As the Singapore dollar appreciated more and later depreciated less compared to other regional currencies (Table 3.2), it raised concerns about Singapore's export competitiveness. This is more pertinent in the cases of Malaysia and Korea, who share a similar export structure to Singapore, especially in the electronics sector.

Singapore is not only trade reliant but its export basket is also concentrated in a few vulnerable products like electronics, which account for nearly 40 per cent of the country's non-oil domestic exports (NODX). According to the Economic Intelligence Unit (EIU), with the onset of the global financial crisis, the importers in developed economies preferred to run down their inventories before placing new orders. Thus, the slump in new orders for computers and related equipment in the United States, coupled with lower income levels elsewhere, adversely affected Singapore's exports. The country's NODX plummeted 35 per cent in January 2009, posting the biggest drop ever on record (Figure 3.3).

Singapore imports also fell, following exports by a few months. The decline in imports reflected the drop in international oil prices and the moderation in domestic

TABLE 3.2
Performance of Regional Currencies
(national currency/USD)

	Singapore	Malaysia	Indonesia	Thailand	Korea	Taiwan	China
Jan 2008–Jun 2008	–5.6	–1.3	–1.7	–0.8	11.6	–6.5	–6.2
Jun 2008–Dec 2008	5.2	6.2	20.5	3.9	20.4	8.0	–0.4

Note: "–" implies appreciation of the national currency.
Source: Author's Calculation.

FIGURE 3.3
Decline in External Trade

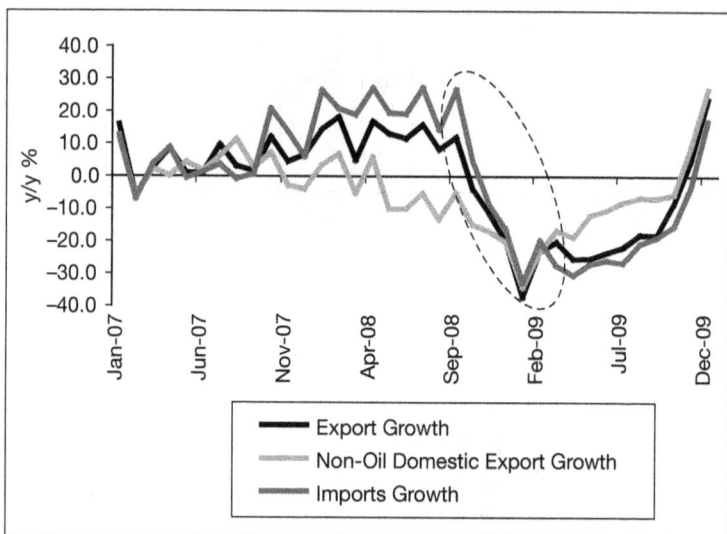

Source: CEIC Database, author's calculation.

economic activity, as well as the growing import intensity of much of the export production.

The rapid contraction of Singapore's GDP was also due to the fact that Singapore is dependent on foreign direct investment (FDI) for supply of capital. Inward FDI accounted for 60.0 per cent of the gross fixed capital formation in the country in 2007. This is in contrast with an average of 9.8 per cent among other Asian economies (excluding Hong Kong). FDI in Singapore plummeted from SG\$7.3 billion to SG\$0.7 billion in the first three quarters of 2008 (Figure 3.4). Lost export revenues reduced income and cast a cloud over investment in export manufacturing.

FIGURE 3.4

Foreign Direct Investment Fell

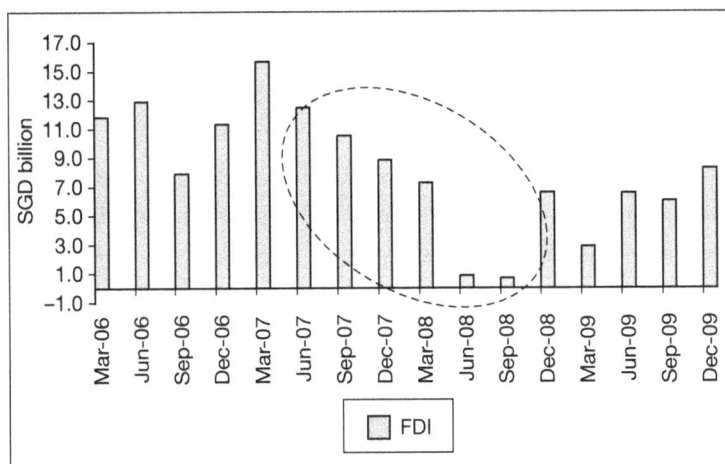

Source: CEIC Database, Singapore Department of Statistics.

Besides trade and investment, Singapore's economy has also been exposed to global shocks through its communication (transportation, logistics), tourism, and other linkages to the rest of the world. This hampered the services sector exports. Entrepôt trade in consumer and capital goods slowed down sharply in Q2-2008 and turned negative in the fourth quarter, reflecting economic uncertainty and the liquidity crunch worldwide. The seaport and airport saw decline in activities and cargo tonnage, and passengers handled contracted in the second half of 2008.

One specific section of the services industry that had a direct impact on the economy and employment was the

Singapore tourism sector. The past decade witnessed a substantial increase in international tourism in the city state, including intra-Asian tourism that reflected the growing prosperity of Asian middle classes as well as some easing of constraints on cross-border travel within the region. However, since the onset of the global financial crisis, there was a steep fall in tourist arrivals in Singapore (Figure 3.5), particularly from the neighbouring nations. People sharply cut down spending on travel and tourism as the crisis severely hit consumer confidence and discretionary spending power. There was also a shift away from high-end tourists to budget travellers, resulting in decline in growth of tourism receipts to 4.8 per cent in 2008 from 14 per cent a year earlier. In addition

FIGURE 3.5
Drop in Tourist Arrivals

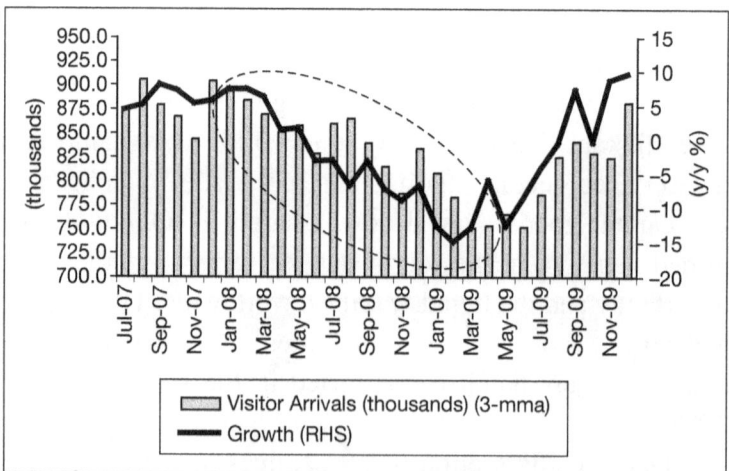

Source: CEIC Database, author's calculation.

to the economic effects of the crisis, concerns about the spread of the H1N1 virus also affected tourist arrivals in the country.

As the economy contracted for most of the year, consumer price inflation (CPI) rose very modestly to just 0.2 per cent in 2009 (Figure 3.6). On the other hand, due to high base effect in 2008, it generated some "disinflation" scenarios for eight months of 2009. External inflationary pressure also remained modest in the second half of 2009 as oil prices hovered around US$70–80 per barrel from the drop in global oil demand. The prices of a number of consumer goods also fell in line with the deteriorating economic environment and negative consumer sentiment.

FIGURE 3.6
Subdued Inflation in Singapore

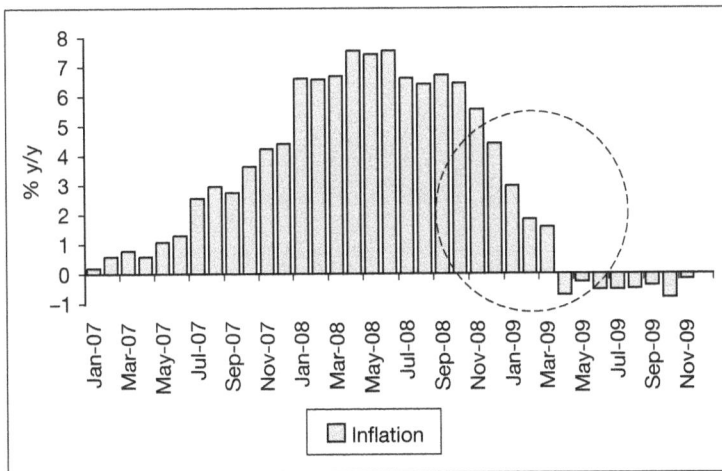

Source: CEIC Database, author's calculation.

Impact on the Financial and Banking Sector

As a small open economy with strong linkages to international events, the Singapore capital market mirrored the sell-offs in the global equity markets. The domestic equity market tumbled from 3500 points in December 2007 to 1700 points in the last quarter of 2008 (Figure 3.7), eroding millions of investor's wealth. Investors from the developed countries withdrew funds to meet challenges at home. As portfolio investment reduced, it became difficult to raise funds in Singapore's domestic capital market. Balance sheets deteriorated for many corporates, adversely

FIGURE 3.7
Stock Market Fell and Currency Depreciated

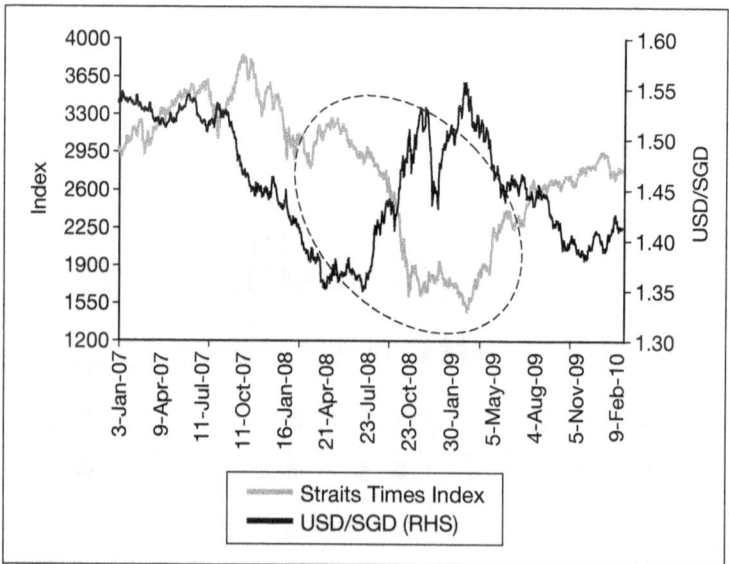

Source: Bloomberg.

affecting the domestic credit market and accentuating the problem of the liquidity crunch.

The crisis also put pressure on the Singapore property market. During the property boom from 2005 to 2008, property prices nearly tripled. While initially the government announced a few measures such as the withdrawal of the deferred payment scheme for residential properties to cool the private residential property market, prices dropped by over 40 per cent from the peak up to mid-2009 as a result of the financial meltdown (Figure 3.8). Falling asset prices have serious implications for property developers, while

FIGURE 3.8

Sharp Fall in Singapore Property Price Index
(private residential)

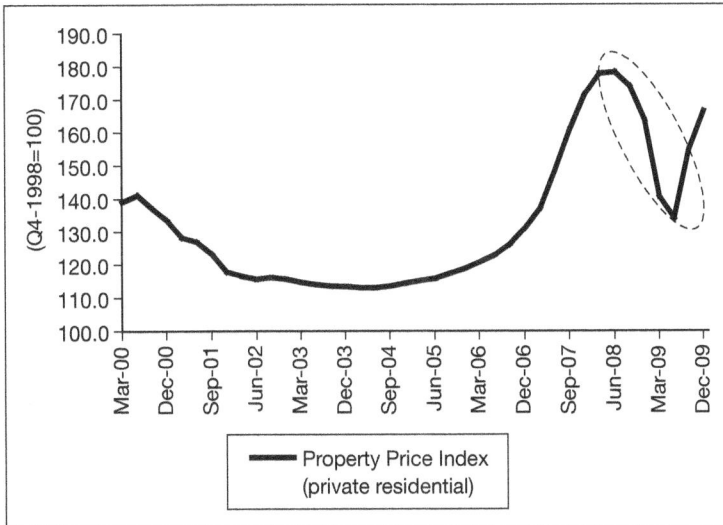

Source: CEIC Database.

the negative wealth effect has repercussions on consumer and investment spending in the country.

The sudden reversal of capital inflows had an effect on liquidity. The Asian Dollar Market experienced strains in tandem with tight liquidity conditions in other U.S. dollar funding centres. The SG$ SIBOR rose in line with US$ LIBOR (Figure 3.9) soon after the disruption in the financial system and failure of Lehman Brothers. The Singapore dollar money market also briefly came under upward pressure on lack of confidence.

Despite withdrawal of funds by foreign investors, Singapore's foreign exchange (FX) market was never a

FIGURE 3.9
Interbank Rates Spiked Briefly

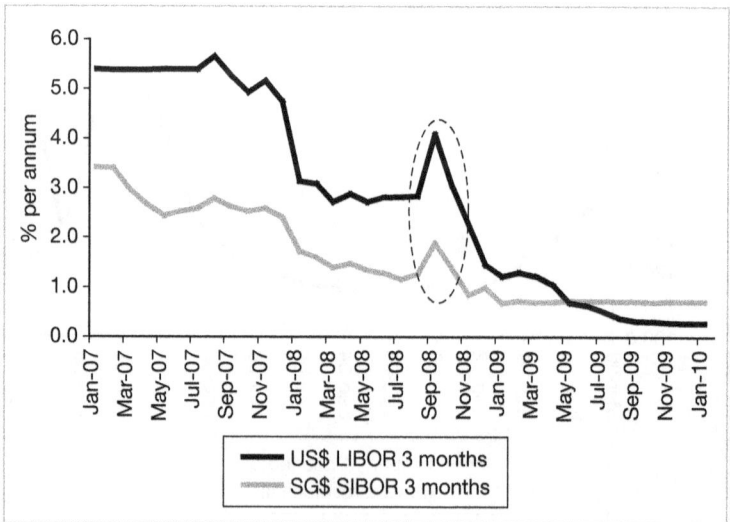

Source: Bloomberg.

serious concern. Though the Singapore dollar depreciated against the U.S. dollar, it was lower than the average of other Asian currencies. SG$ NEER (nominal effective exchange rate) was well supported at the lower bound of the estimated MAS policy band.[1] This stability can be attributed to Singapore's huge foreign reserves, which act as a safeguard against speculative activities on the Singapore dollar. Singapore's official reserves held by the MAS stood at SG$264 billion at the end of December 2009. On top of this, there are the twin sovereign wealth funds (SWFs) — Government Investment Corporation (GIC) and Temasek Holdings — which have assets of more than US$200 billion (IMF, *GFSR* 2007).

The damage to Singapore's banking sector had remained contained, given its very low level of exposure to securities linked to U.S. home mortgages or to distressed financial institutions like Bear Stearns and Lehman Brothers. The immediate impact of the financial meltdown was mainly in terms of depressed share prices (Figure 3.10) as they fell by more than 50 per cent from the peak.

However, by late 2008, the global economic downturn slowed business activities, thus reducing demand for loans. Also banks became more cautious and in their effort to shore up capital adequacy they turned down riskier borrowers, including SMEs. Overall Asian currency units (ACU) lending contracted 16 per cent between its October 2008 peak and September 2009 and total domestic banking units (DBU) lending fell in Q3-2009 (Figure 3.11). The risk premium also increased as banks became more cautious amid weakened corporate performance during economic uncertainty. As loan delinquencies and non-performing

FIGURE 3.10

Drop in Local Banks' Share Prices

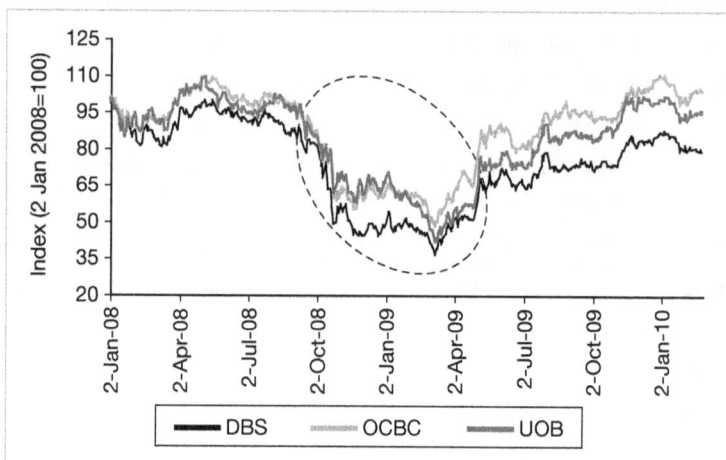

Source: Bloomberg, author's calculation.

FIGURE 3.11

Less Demand for Loans and Advances

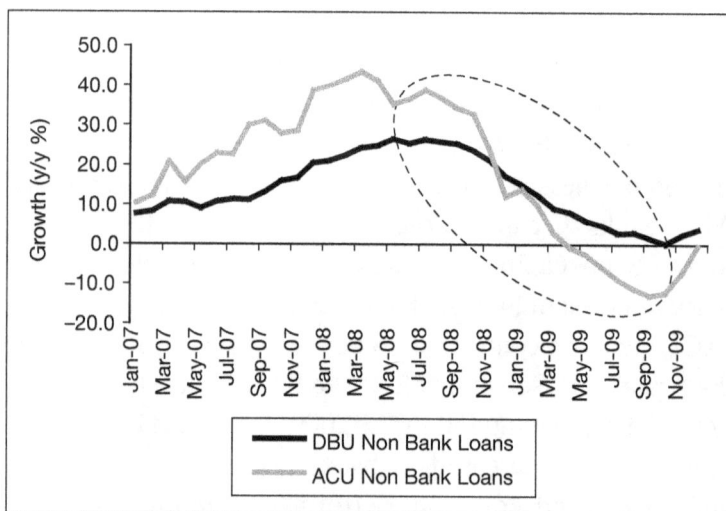

Source: CEIC Database, author's calculation.

loans (NPLs) caused the economy to lag, the banking system's NPL ratio started to deteriorate only in the later part of 2008 (Figure 3.12).

Nevertheless, having entered the crisis from a position of strength, the banking sector profitability indicators showed resiliency (Figure 3.13). Unlike the banking system in the United States and the European Union, local banks had not recorded any threatening losses and there was no need for any government bailout. The local banks were also comfortably placed in face of further downside risks. This is reflected in the Tier-1 Capital Adequacy Ratio (CAR), which now averages 13.5 per cent, well above the MAS's regulatory requirements (Figure 3.14).

FIGURE 3.12
NPL Ratio Deteriorated from Q4-2008

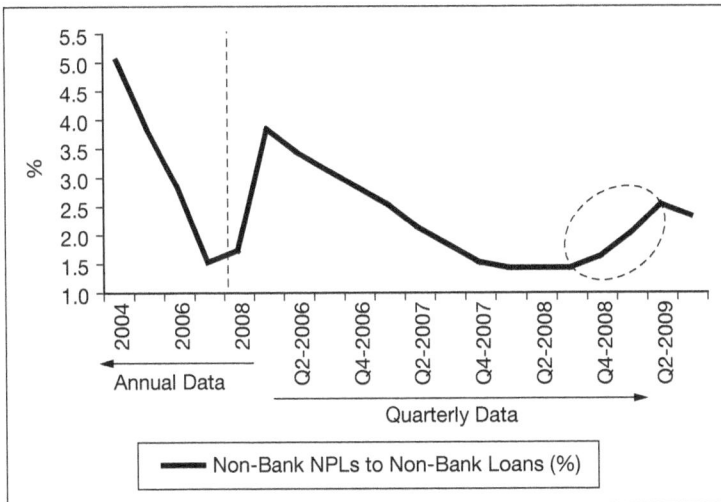

Source: MAS *Financial Stability Review* (various issues).

FIGURE 3.13
Profitability Indicators Showed Resiliency

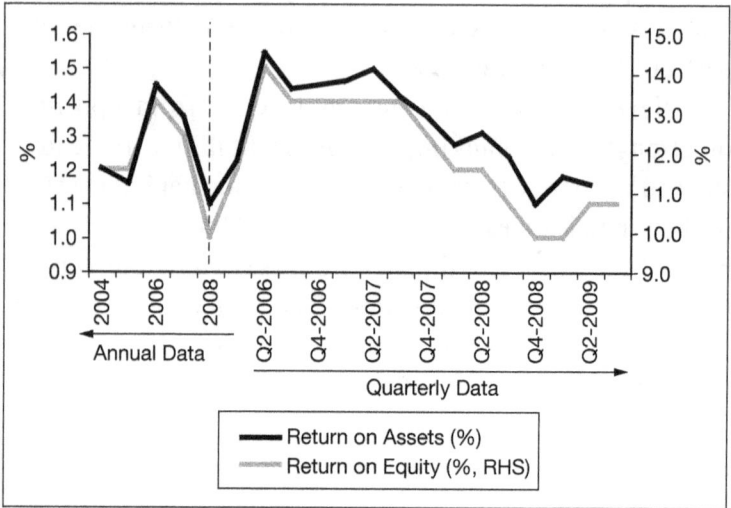

Source: MAS *Financial Stability Review* (various issues).

FIGURE 3.14
CARs above MAS's Regulatory Requirement

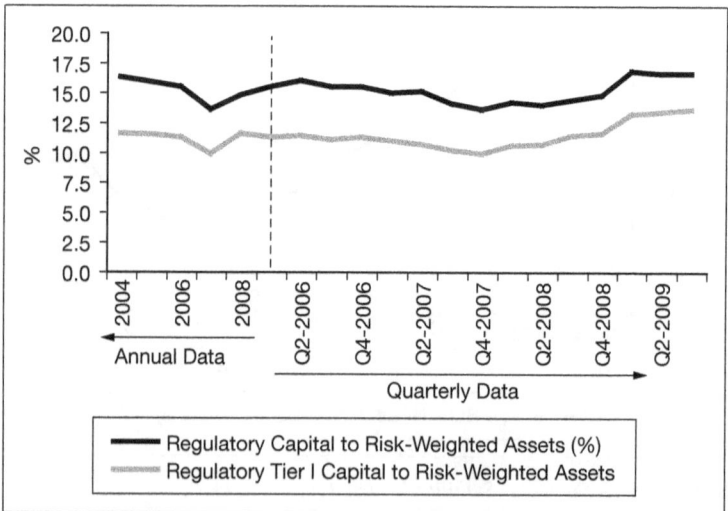

Source: MAS *Financial Stability Review* (various issues).

Impact on the labour market

During the 2008 crisis the Singapore labour market weakened towards the end of the year. The main source of the weakness emerged from the manufacturing sector, specifically electronics, as the global slowdown dried up demand for manufactured exports, which in turn forced companies to reduce headcount and lower the cost of operation.

The crisis affected the workers in Singapore in two ways. First, there was loss of employment, either through complete job loss or a temporary reduction in the number of working days; secondly, there was downward pressure on wages. This affected workers in export industries (such as electronics) and the tourism industry as well as migrant workers. The workers were also indirectly affected by the adverse linkage effects of the primary employment reduction. The group included self-employed workers and those working in casual activities to supply goods and services within the domestic economy. The crisis was a severe blow mainly for individuals who were already having trouble finding and keeping jobs. The low-skilled immigrants were among the first to suffer because they were concentrated in vulnerable sectors such as construction and tourism and often held jobs on contract.

Economic data shows that the labour market softened in the second half of 2008 and job creation slowed to 21,300 in Q4-2008, less than half the number of jobs created in Q3. Firms' cost-cutting efforts, banking sector uncertainty, and delay and cancellation of investment projects weighed on

Singapore's 2.9 million strong labour force. Nevertheless, the deterioration in the labour market was far more modest compared to past recessions. During the Asian Financial Crisis in 1998 and the global IT downturn in 2001, employment began to fall three quarters after the peak in GDP. In comparison, in the current economic cycle, which peaked in Q1-2008, employment growth remained positive for four quarters. Even in the first quarter of 2009, the net drop in employment was much smaller compared to similar stages in earlier recessions.

The greater resilience of the labour market compared with past economic downturns could be attributed to the construction and services sectors. The construction sector, with big projects like Marina Bay Financial Centre, integrated resorts (IRs), MRT Downtown Line, and Marina Coastal Expressway, have lifted demand for construction workers. The services sector was largely supported by the upcoming IRs, together with the completion of new shopping malls, which created jobs mainly in the retail trade and hotels and restaurants. However, the expansion in headcount was 40 per cent less compared to an average quarterly gain in the first three quarters of 2008.

In tandem with the weakening labour market, retrenchments jumped almost five times to 10,000 in Q1-2009 from a year earlier (Figure 3.15). Apart from manufacturing, which accounted for more than 70 per cent of retrenchments in Q1-2009, the services sector also displaced a large number of workers (Figure 3.16).

Given this scenario, the overall unemployment rate edged up to a high of 3.4 per cent in September 2009, although it was only half the 6.2 per cent peak

FIGURE 3.15
Retrenchment Peaked in Early 2009

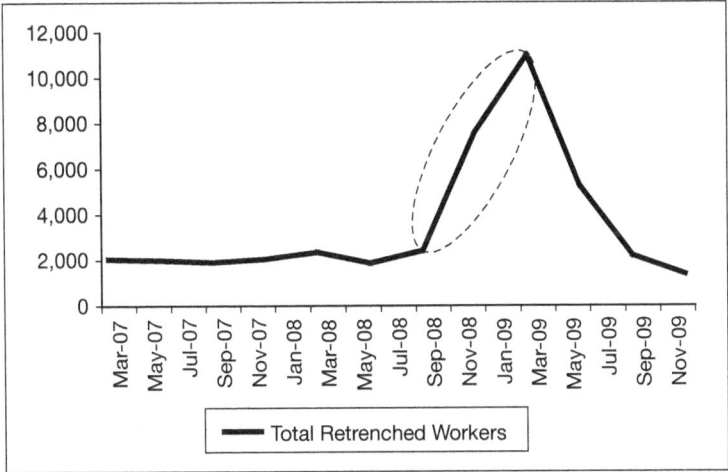

Source: CEIC Database.

FIGURE 3.16
Highest Retrenchment in Manufacturing

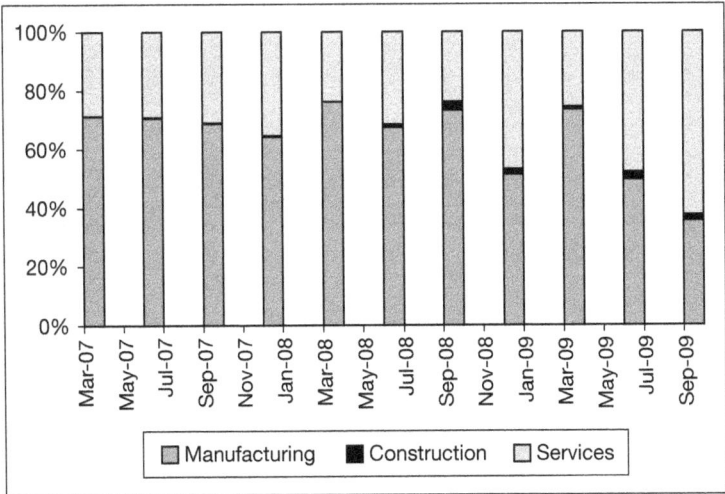

Source: CEIC Database.

in September 2003. The resident unemployment rate, a more accurate measure for the local population, climbed to a seasonally adjusted 5.0 per cent in September 2009 from 3.4 per cent a year ago (Figure 3.17). The increase in the unemployment rate largely reflected the slowdown in employment growth.

FIGURE 3.17
Rise in Unemployment Rate

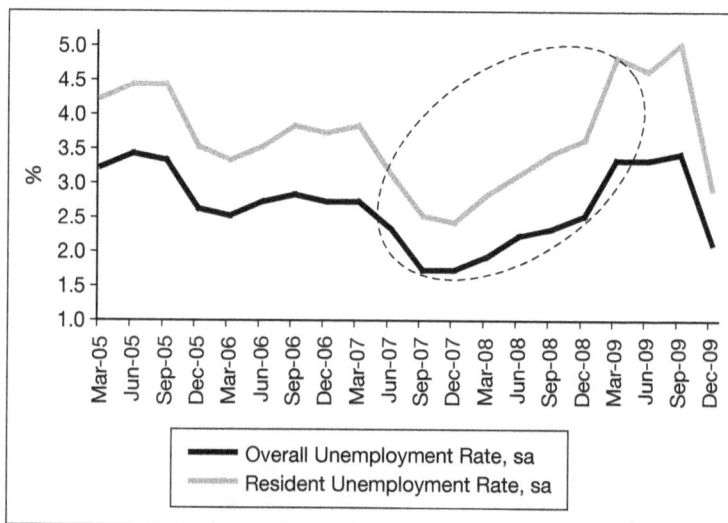

Source: CEIC Database.

Strengths of the Singapore Economy

Despite several setbacks from the global economic crisis, Singapore still remains one of the economies with a tough foundation. Although it never created a recession on its own, it has proven itself time and again in every global or regional recession. This is mainly because of the following factors.

Strong Macroeconomic Fundamentals

Singapore stands out in any difficult test as it has strong macroeconomic fundamentals. Real GDP growth has been high and sustained around 7.5 per cent just before the crisis emerged. It has robust foreign exchange reserves and a large current account surplus (Table 3.3). Good corporate governance and the credibility of policymakers have always helped to maintain Singapore's attraction. The sound economic fundamentals of the economy have been supported by a well-supervised banking sector

TABLE 3.3

Selected Economic Indicators of Singapore

	2005	2006	2007
Real Economy			
GDP Growth Rate (%)	7.3	8.4	7.8
Gross National Savings (% of GDP)	43.0	45.0	44.0
Gross Capital Formation (% of GDP)	20.0	20.0	21.0
Inflation (%)	0.5	1.0	2.1
Public Finance			
Government Surplus (% of GDP)	6.5	9.5	11.5
Balance of Payment			
Current Account Balance (% of GDP)	23.0	25.0	24.0
Overall Balance (% of GDP)	10.0	12.0	11.5
Official Foreign Reserves (SG$ bn)	193	209	235

Source: *Yearbook of Statistics*, 2009, Singapore Department of Statistics.

(Table 3.4). The banks are also well-capitalized as the required capital (also known as Tier-I capital) that banks are supposed to hold averaged 11.3 per cent, which is nearly three times the Bank of International Settlements' (BIS) recommendation of 4 per cent and well above the MAS's 6 per cent minimum.

The strong economic and banking fundamentals was also one of the factors that helped Singapore to survive the crisis with the minimum glitches. Even when the numbers were depicting the worst recession in the city state's history,

TABLE 3.4

Selected Indicators on Banking Sector Financial Soundness

	2005	2006	2007
Liquidity			
Liquid DBU Assets to Total DBU Assets	10.3	9.8	10.1
DBU Non-bank Loans to DBU Non-Bank Deposits	81.8	71.4	74.1
Capital Adequacy (%)			
Regulatory Capital to Risk-Weighted Assets	15.8	15.4	13.5
Regulatory Tier I Capital to Risk-Weighted Assets	11.4	11.2	9.8
Asset Quality (%)			
Non-bank NPLs to Non-Bank loans (%)	3.8	2.8	1.5
Total Provisions to Non-Bank NPLs	78.7	89.5	115.6
Profitability (%)			
ROA (simple average)	1.2	1.4	1.3
ROE (simple average)	11.2	13.7	12.9

Source: *MAS Financial Stability Review*, November 2008.

there were some facts which presented a different picture. While retail sales dropped by 15 per cent in January 2009, it was still better than the 20 per cent plunge during the 1997–98 financial crisis. The property prices stabilized and in some cases inched up very quickly. Visible consumer consumption did not seem to have declined as much as the crisis implied. The reason for a disconnect between statistics and the picture on the ground was that Singapore entered the 2008 recession from a position of strength. In particular, the two years preceding the downturn saw high economic growth that boosted workers' average monthly earnings by 5.8 per cent a year. This provided some assistance to the Singapore population as they drew down from their past incomes and muted the blows of the financial crisis. Moreover, Singapore has a large proportion of foreign workers and expatriates and it was their employment that was the first to go when the crisis hit. But programmes like the Jobs Credit Scheme which was announced by the government (discussed in Chapter 4) in the wake of the crisis helped to protect the local workers. Thus, while foreigners suffered most of the losses, the spill-over to the locals was comparatively contained, which portrayed a less-than-disastrous state of the real economy.

Exchange Rate Management System

The MAS manages the Singapore dollar through a "basket system". It manages the NEER, which is allowed to move (with moderate fluctuations) within an undisclosed target band consistent with Singapore's economic fundamentals. That is why even in the 1997–98 financial crisis when its neighbouring countries suffered from a serious currency crisis, the Singapore dollar remained stable. This time again, Singapore's NEER remained within the policy band amid continued capital outflows.

Adjustable Wage System

The wage system in Singapore is fairly flexible, as it allows for wage reductions in difficult times. The National Wages Council (NWC) sets annual wage guidelines in light of external market pressures and domestic inflationary concerns. The pay structure recommended by NWC comprises a basic wage and a monthly variable component (MVC). It also consists of an annual wage supplement (AWS) and an annual variable bonus. While the MVC allows for quick adjustments to wage costs, the AWS and annual variable bonus allow cuts in year-end bonus, annual wage supplement, or Central Provident Fund (CPF) contribution rates. This is a very useful system as it helps to reduce business cost by cutting wages, while maintaining the same number of headcount during an economic downturn.

Summing up

With increasing integration of the Singapore economy and its financial markets with the rest of the world, it is indeed not surprising that the country faces significant downside risks from any international shocks. As a result, alongside the deterioration in the external environment, the Singapore economy weakened markedly in the second half of 2008 and early 2009. It ran into recession following the near-collapse of the global financial system. Due to reversal of portfolio equity flows, the domestic equity market experienced sharp declines and incurred huge losses. The concomitant effect was felt in the economy's liquidity conditions. However, damage to the banking sector remained contained. The drag on the global economy also presented challenges for the Singapore labour market, although the extent of retrenchments was far more modest compared to past recessions.

Despite the adverse impacts triggered by the global crisis, Singapore's fundamentals continued to remain strong. Its strong economic base, healthy banking sector, unique FX management system, and adjustable wage structure give it enough ammunition to ride any international shocks.

Notes

1. Since 1981, monetary policy in Singapore has been centred on the management of the exchange rate. There are no independent targets for money supply growth or interest rates. The Singapore dollar is managed against a trade-weighted basket of currencies of Singapore's major trading partners and competitors. The MAS operates a managed float regime for the Singapore dollar. The trade-weighted exchange rate is allowed to fluctuate within a policy band. The band provides a mechanism to accommodate short-term fluctuations in the foreign exchange markets and flexibility in managing the exchange rate.

4
Singapore's Policy Responses to the Global Economic Crisis

For Singapore, the recession came mainly through the fall in non-oil exports and output. The monetary and financial systems for the city state largely remained unscathed. The financial shocks were mostly felt through drying up of credit and capital flows due to heightened risk aversion. But, apart from these initial stresses, there were no severe financial dislocations. Inflation and exchange rates remained stable. This was also enunciated by Finance Minister Tharman Shanmugaratnam in his speech while presenting the 2009 budget in Parliament on 22 January 2009. He stated that the key risk facing Singapore was the scale of the recession and loss of jobs rather than inflation.

Hence Singapore carved out policies that could cushion businesses and households from the impact of the economic downturn, maintain confidence in the financial market, and support economic recovery in the long-run.

Policymakers' Objective

The success of Singapore coming out of the crisis depended on the country's policy responses at both the domestic and regional levels. Being a small open economy, the conventional fiscal and monetary policies to boost domestic demand were not very effective. The city state's private consumption and investment have been highly dependent on export demand. Hence, the MAS used the exchange rate mechanism to gradually respond to the external demand shocks that confronted the economy during the intense phase of the crisis. The central bank also aimed for a low inflationary environment and ensured that the Singapore dollar remained an anchor of stability.

Similarly, the FY2009 budget aimed at the supply side of the economy, more particularly in keeping jobs. This was mainly due to Singapore being a significant consumer of imports (import to GDP ratio was more than 200 per cent in 2007 vis-à-vis an average of 81 per cent in Asia), so demand-boosting stimulus measures would be challenged by import leakages.

The policymakers also worked cautiously in tandem with other regional initiatives to preserve confidence in the financial system, which had been wrecked by the huge losses suffered by some of the biggest banks in the United States and the European Union. The government, through its expansionary fiscal measures, also initiated several long-term structural reforms (like increasing labour productivity) and tried to position the country better for an upturn in the economy.

Policy Responses

Measures to Stabilize Financial and Banking System

While the financial system in Singapore had remained stable and robust, the government took a few precautionary measures to maintain confidence in the country's financial and banking system. On 16 October 2008, the Singapore Government announced a blanket guarantee on deposits of individuals and non-bank customers in banks, finance companies, and merchant banks licensed by the MAS. This was in line with a number of other countries in Asia — Taiwan, Hong Kong, Malaysia, and Indonesia — and was aimed to ensure a level international playing field for banks in Singapore. The guarantee, which would be effective until 31 December 2010, was to be backed by more than SG\$200 billion of the reserves of the Singapore Government.

Following the collapse of Lehman Brothers in September 2008, money markets globally came under pressure. While the Singapore dollar money markets stayed relatively calm, it could not remain immune to the global dislocations due to Singapore's openness in the financial system. Thus, to ensure the smooth functioning of financial markets, the MAS assured easy accessibility of Singapore dollar and U.S. dollar to all financial institutions. It enhanced the liquidity in the system in two ways: (a) It maintained a higher level of Singapore dollar liquidity in the banking system; and (b) entered into a precautionary US\$30 billion swap arrangement with the U.S. Federal Reserve.

Being the largest U.S. dollar and foreign exchange centre in Asia outside of Japan, it was important for MAS to avoid any critical seizure experienced by other funding markets in the world. Thus, as a precautionary measure, it established the US$30 billion swap line with the U.S. Federal Reserve on 30 October 2008 and joined thirteen other major central banks from Australia to Brazil, from Europe to Asia, to have such a facility with the U.S. central bank. The facility, which was initially till April 2009, was later extended to February 2010. According to the MAS, the swap line would enhance confidence in the robustness of the Asian Dollar Market for U.S. dollar funding and in the resilience of the foreign exchange markets in Singapore.

In addition, in July 2008, the MAS expanded the Standing Facility to include all participating banks of the MAS Electronic Payment System (MEPS). This provided banks with the assurance that they would be able to access central bank liquidity if the need arose.

Monetary Policy Measures

The MAS conducts monetary policy by targeting the exchange rate and not by setting the interest rates. The SG$ NEER is used to achieve the twin economic objectives of high growth and stable, low inflation. During the crisis, the main concern facing the MAS was how to moderate the economic slowdown. Hence, unlike other countries where policy rates were slashed to support economic growth, the city state used the NEER to steer the economy.

With the onset of the global financial crisis, the MAS's immediate response was to abandon its four-year-long strong Singapore dollar policy. At its policy review meeting on 10 October 2008, the policy stance was shifted to zero appreciation (or neutral bias) for the country's effective exchange rate. Although this was not enough to counteract fully the global slump, it helped to soften the blow from external headwinds and shore up confidence among the stakeholders in the country (Figure 4.1).

In early 2009, Singapore faced a more ominous situation compared to 2008. During the monetary policy meeting on 14 April 2009, the MAS maintained its neutral

FIGURE 4.1

MAS Maintaining a Neutral Exchange Rate Policy Stance

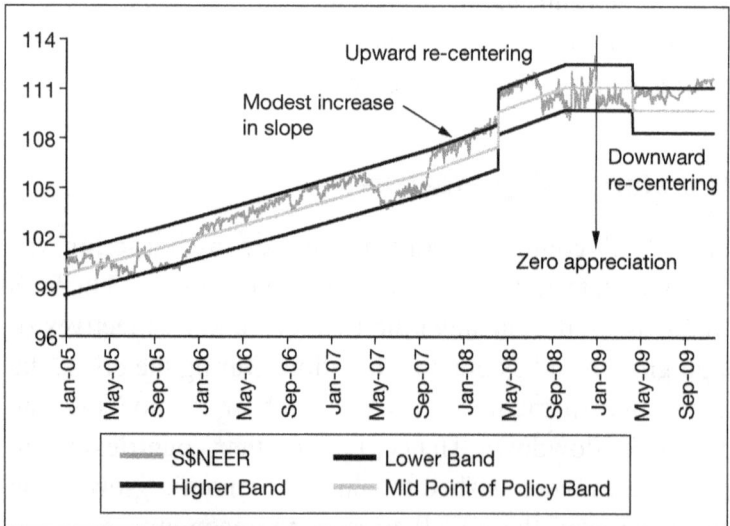

Source: Bloomberg, author's calculation.

FX stance but re-centred the policy band at the prevailing level of the SG$ NEER. As the SG$ was trading around 0.5 per cent away from the floor of the policy band ahead of the meeting, the central bank reversed the estimated 1.5 per cent tightening made back in April 2008. Thereafter, the MAS did not ease monetary policy further by shifting to a SG$ NEER depreciation stance or widening the trading band, as such steps could have led to more volatility in SG$ movements (Appendix I).

Fiscal Policy Measures

Amid heightened uncertainty, Singapore offered an unprecedented fiscal stimulus package (Appendix II). The Finance Minister brought forward the date of announcement of the budget to January 2009 instead of February, realizing the urgent need of government support to ride out the economic downturn. Even before that, immediate measures were put in place in November 2008 to help local firms which were hurt by the global credit constraints. On 22 January 2009, the Finance Minister delivered a SG$20.5 billion "Resilience Package" for FY2009 with the main focus to boost employability of people. For the first time, the government dug into its reserves to draw SG$4.9 billion to fund two temporary and innovative measures (Jobs Credit Scheme and Special Risk-Sharing Initiative).

The traditional stance of basic budget balance, excluding the transfers to endowment funds as well as the contributions from net investment returns, was abandoned for a large deficit of SG$14.9 billion in FY2009 (6.0 per cent of GDP). This was markedly larger than a revised deficit of SG$2.8 billion in FY2008 (1.1 per cent of GDP).[1] The revised overall budget balance for FY2009 was estimated to be a deficit of SG$8.7 billion (3.5 per cent of GDP) (Table 4.1).

The Resilience Package contained a diversified set of targeted measures, with multiple impact points for workers, households, and businesses. It went into five main areas: SG$5.1 billion to preserving jobs; SG$5.8 billion to stimulate bank lending; SG$2.6 billion for various tax measures to improve cash flow of businesses; SG$2.6 billion to help households through moves like personal income tax rebates; SG$4.4 billion to bring forward infrastructure spending plus health and education improvements (Box 4.1).

BOX 4.1
Resilience Package

The Resilience Package had five components consisting of:

1. Jobs for Singaporeans

To help Singaporeans stay employed, the government decided to spend SG$5.1 billion by:

- Introducing the Jobs Credit Scheme
- Enhancing the Skills Programme for Upgrading and Resilience (SPUR)
- Providing the Workfare Income Supplement (WIS) Special Payment
- Expanding recruitment across the public sector

2. Stimulating Bank Lending

To ensure that viable companies continue to have access to credit to sustain their operations and keep jobs, the government announced it would spend SG$5.8 billion to stimulate bank lending by:

- Enhancing existing bank lending schemes
- Introducing the Special Risk-Sharing Initiative (SRI) comprising a new bridging loan programme and risk-sharing schemes for trade financing

3. Enhancing Business Cash flow and Competitiveness

The government also came up with a SG$2.6 billion expenditure plan to support business cash-flow and strengthen Singapore's competitiveness through:

- Tax concessions and measures
- Easing cash-flow and sharpening Singapore's competitiveness

4. Supporting Families

SG$2.6 billion was set aside in the budget to provide additional support for families and communities during the 2009 downturn through:

- Direct assistance for Singaporean households
- Increased targeted help for vulnerable groups
- Additional support for charitable giving and the community

5. Building a Home for the Future

The government is expected to spend SG$4.4 billion to develop Singapore as a global-city and best-home for Singaporeans by:

- Bringing forward infrastructure projects
- Rejuvenating public housing estates
- Enhancing sustainable development programmes
- Upgrading education and health infrastructure

Source: Singapore Budget 2009, Ministry of Finance, Singapore.

TABLE 4.1

Singapore Budget Statistics (as of 22 January 2009)

SG$ billion	FY2003	FY2004	FY2005	FY2006	FY2007	FY2008 (Revised)	FY2009 (Budget)
Operating Revenue	25.3	27.5	28.2	31.3	40.4	40.5	33.4
Taxes and Fees	25.0	27.2	27.9	31.0	40.2	40.3	33.2
Total Expenditure	28.5	28.9	28.6	29.9	32.9	38.9	43.6
Operating Expenditure	20.0	20.4	21.4	23.9	25.9	29.2	32.1
Development Expenditure	8.5	8.6	7.2	5.9	7.0	9.6	11.5
Primary Budget Balance*	-3.2	-1.5	-0.5	1.4	7.4	1.6	-10.2
As % of GDP	-1.9	-0.8	-0.2	0.6	2.9	0.6	-4.1
Less: Special Transfers	0.5	1.7	0.8	3.6	2.1	7.4	6.1
Basic Balance**	-3.7	-2.4	-1.0	-1.2	6.0	-2.8	-14.9
As % of GDP	-2.3	-2.3	-0.5	-0.6	2.4	-1.1	-6.0
Add: NII Contribution	1.9	3.0	2.8	2.1	2.4	3.6	7.7
Overall Budget Balance	-1.9	-0.1	1.5	-0.06	7.6	-2.1	-8.7
As % of GDP	-1.1	-0.1	0.7	0.0	3.1	-0.8	-3.5

Note: "–" implies deficit. Figures may not add up due to rounding.
*Surplus (deficit) before special transfers, endowment fund top-ups, and net investment income (NII) contribution.
**Excludes endowment fund top-ups and NII.
Source: Ministry of Finance.

Indeed, the Resilience Package announced by the government was all-encompassing as it tried to help both corporates and citizens to cope with the economic slowdown. While on one hand it strived to meet companies' financial needs, on the other hand it aimed to soothe the pain that Singaporeans felt from the crisis.

One of the main objectives of the FY2009 budget was to preserve jobs and in that regard the introduction of the Job Credit Scheme (JCS) deserves special mention (Box 4.2). The initiative, which was expected to lower the cost of hires for companies, was estimated to take up more than half of the SG$6.1 billion in special transfers earmarked for FY2009. Under this, employers received a 12 per cent cash grant on the first SG$2,500 of each month's wages for each employee on their CPF payroll.

BOX 4.2

Job Credit Scheme Helped to Lessen Impact on Job Cuts

Singapore policymakers announced an unprecedented Jobs Credit scheme (JCS) of SG$4.5 billion in the FY2009 budget to prevent mass layoffs. The JCS was a cash grant to employers to reduce their costs of employing Singaporean workers during the crisis. The cash grant was equivalent to 12 per cent of the first SG$2,500 of the wages of each employee who contributes to the CPF, the national savings plan. It equated to a 9 percentage point cut in the employers' CPF contribution rate. This was given in four quarterly payments, with each payment based on the employees who were with the employer at that time.

For instance, a worker whose wage was SG$2,500 meant that the employer received SG$900 a quarter, or SG$300 a month. The scheme, which was initially rolled out for a year, was later extended for six months with graduated payments of 6 per cent of wages in March 2010 and 3 per cent in June 2010 respectively.

Essentially, JCS was a temporary employment subsidization programme that was expected to directly help companies shoulder part of their wage costs and encourage them to retain workers in the downturn. It was to help competitive firms to hold on to skilled and experienced workers, in preparation for an economic upturn. Another consequence of JCS would include stimulation in demand through a multiplier effect. But the impact in this case would be much smaller as demand stimulation in Singapore is of limited utility, due to the high leakage in the open economy.

The first payment of the Jobs Credit was made on 31 March 2009, when 100,000 employers with 1.3 million local staff received SG$920 million to help them through the economic downturn. The key factors that allowed the government to implement the plan quickly and efficiently were: (a) the robust CPF database in place to determine the wages of employees and (b) standardized identification numbers for each of the 385,000 businesses registered in Singapore — known as Unique Entity Numbers (UEN) — that helped to easily match the existing records held by different government agencies. While any government assistance scheme could be complex and multifaceted with numerous policy and implementation considerations, in the case of Singapore, different government agencies worked together on their respective strengths to implement the policy effectively and efficiently.

Anecdotal evidence indicated that the savings and additional cash flow from the JCS were quite significant, especially for labour-intensive firms, and helped to save some jobs. Another empirical analysis found that the programme was capable of saving up to 30,000 jobs in 2009, and 50,000 each in 2010 and 2011. Thus, had the scheme been not introduced, the GDP contraction would have led to larger job reductions over a longer period of time.

Besides Jobs Credit, course fee subsidies under the Skills Programme for Upgrading and Resilience (SPUR) was increased from 80 per cent to 90 per cent. Selected tertiary courses at UniSIM and Singapore's three public universities were included under SPUR. The EDB was expected to complement SPUR with a SG$100 million programme. All this was believed to help new graduates and PMETs (professionals, managers, executives, and technicians) to upgrade themselves to allow them to find jobs with ease in the future.

During this downturn, some low-income workers faced lower wages or even fewer working hours, which implied a smaller take-home pay. To help this segment of the labour force, the government decided to adjust the Workfare Income Supplement (WIS) with an additional 50 per cent payment. In addition to a SG$200 increase in monthly salary of SG$1,000, the worker received another SG$600. The government also relaxed the eligibility criteria for the Workfare Special Payment to include odd-job workers. In all, the temporary Workfare Income Supplement Special Payment was expected to cost the government SG$150 million.

The government also announced plans to create 18,000 jobs in the public sector and government-supported sectors including childcare, tertiary education, and restructured hospitals. This was planned to be implemented over two years so as to help absorb new graduates and cushion unemployment.

Besides minimizing job losses and creating employment, the government also looked at enhancing the competitiveness of businesses. It cut the corporate income tax rate by 1 percentage point to 17 per cent from Year of Assessment (YA) 2010 to maintain Singapore's attractiveness as a location for investments. This lower tax rate would be more comparable with Hong Kong's 16.5 per cent (Figure 4.2).

FIGURE 4.2
Singapore Corporate Rate Tax

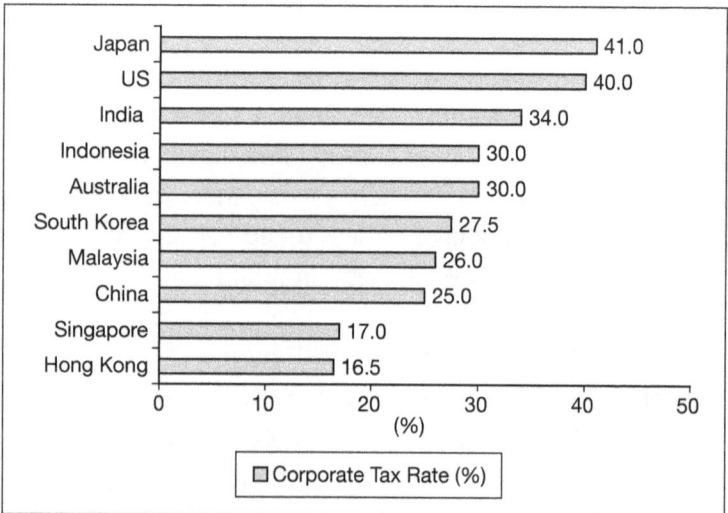

Source: Budget Highlights, FY2009, Ministry of Finance, Singapore.

In response to the global credit crunch, the Singapore Government decided to take on a significant share in the risks of bank lending. It introduced the Special Risk-Sharing Initiative (SRI) so as to ensure that viable companies continue to have access to credit to sustain operations and minimize job dismissals. The SRI comprised a new Bridging Loan Programme (BLP) and trade financing schemes. The new BLP was expected to extend government support to a broader segment of the credit market, particularly mid-sized companies (Box 4.3).

BOX 4.3
Special Risk-Sharing Initiative Encouraged Business Financing

Besides job preservation, in the FY2009 budget, the government also pointed to another key area of focus: freeing up credit for companies. To achieve this, it introduced the Special Risk-Sharing Initiative (SRI), which allowed companies, both MNCs and SMEs alike, to obtain funds during the 2008 credit crunch. This initiative had two components and was introduced for one year. The government extended the scheme in December 2009 till end January 2011.

New Bridging Loan Programme (BLP)

The BLP had been enhanced to cater to loans of up to SG$5 million, up from SG$500,000. The government raised its share of risk on these loans to 80 per cent, up from the previous 50 per cent. This was expected to meet the working capital needs of most small to mid-sized firms, as well as some bigger ones. The new BLP was applicable for all new loans from 1 February 2009, and included refinancing of existing loans when they were due. The scheme catered to loans of up to four years maturity.

Trade Financing

To address constraints to limited private insurance capacity and a reduced risk appetite, the government, for the first time, decided to take on a significant share of the risk in trade financing. This was important for companies that had existing orders and who needed loans to fulfil their orders as well as insurance against the risk of their buyers defaulting on payments. The new trade finance schemes were expected to help mid-sized and large exporters obtain loans and trade insurance on the scale they needed.

The Finance Minister also extended the tax deduction on loss provisions made pursuant to MAS Notice 612 for banks, as well as other equivalent MAS notices for finance companies and merchant banks, for three years of assessment. This was likely to "encourage banks to continue making adequate loan impairment provisions and bolster their financial strength to underpin continued lending in the downturn".

When the SRI and other business financing schemes were announced in January 2009, the government expected the banks to take advantage of the schemes and play their part to ensure that viable companies received adequate funding to ride out the crisis. It was believed that the scheme could lead to SG$11 billion of loans in 2009, of which SG$5.8 billion would be government capital. By the end of 2009, the government met most of its expectations. The SRI and the enhancement schemes catalysed more than 14,000 loans worth about SG$8 billion. More than 13,000 companies, of which 90 per cent were SMEs, have benefited from the scheme. Moreover, the total amount of loans given was about 5.5 times more than the loan amount given out under the government-assisted schemes over the one-year period prior to the changes.

After extending the SRI scheme till end-January 2011, the government expects to support up to SG$8.4 billion of new loans. While previously the SRI scheme was funded from Singapore's past reserves, with a better economic outlook in 2010, the government has decided to fund the extension from its regular budget.

The property market has also been bolstered with several measures. These included a 40 per cent property tax rebate for commercial assets and deferred property tax for approved development land. These were likely to enable property developers to hold back on their intended developments. Property tax for the higher-valued secondary home was scrapped so as to prevent fire sales of high-end properties in the market.

In addition to measures to boost employability and help corporates to stay afloat, the Singapore Government also offered a slew of measures to alleviate the pain of the households. It infused SG$2.6 billion directly to lessen hardships of Singaporeans. The government announced a personal income tax rebate of 20 per cent (capped at SG$2,000) in FY2009. It also doubled the Goods and Services Tax (GST) credits for households in FY2009. Low-income earners and the elderly also gained in the form of increased allowances, service and conservancy rebates, and topping up of their ElderCare Fund and Medifund.

The 40 per cent property tax rebate for owner-occupied residential properties was expected to also take away additional costs for households. However, to ensure that first time homebuyers could afford public housing, the government also increased the additional CPF housing grant by SG$10,000 to SG$40,000.

In order to pump-prime the economy, Singapore in its FY2009 Budget also increased public sector construction spending significantly, with SG$18 billion to SG$20 billion worth of contracts expected to go ahead. This compares with SG$15 billion in FY2008 and SG$6 billion in FY2007. Many smaller projects (up to a value of SG$50 million each) were brought forward. Some of these projects included Housing Development Board (HDB) lift upgrading, school upgrading, park connectors, and military facilities as well as sewage and drainage projects. These initiatives were targeted to help the smaller firms within the construction industry that were reeling under the economic slowdown.

Thus, while there was little the government could do to counteract the serious decline in external demand, it definitely assisted both companies and households to survive the crisis. In Tharman Shanmugaratnam's words, "The Resilience Package will not get us out of the recession, as long as the global economy continues to contract, but it will help avert an even sharper downturn, and more lasting damage to the economy."

Regional Response

Singapore is also part of ASEAN's response mechanism to the global economic crisis. The current crisis strengthens the justification for establishing an ASEAN Economic Community (AEC) by 2015. The "single market and production base" promised under AEC is expected to provide a highly competitive economic region to attract FDIs and facilitate greater trade flows in the region.

The global economic crisis also gave the members of the ASEAN Plus Three group an opportunity to intensify their acts under financial cooperation. In May 2009, in order to build-up confidence in the region, the Finance Ministers of ASEAN Plus Three agreed on the implementation plan for the multilateralization of the CMI and expand their commitments to a total of US$120 billion from US$90 billion. They also planned to expand the local currency bond market as a source of investment and finance for the region. All these initiatives were mainly taken to fend off any financial crisis.

Assessment of Policy Responses

Singapore's policy responses to the global economic crisis have been timely and practical. For an immediate remedy the exchange rate adjustment was used to cushion the rapidly decelerating output. Later, expansionary fiscal and cost-cutting measures were implemented to help companies with their balance sheets and arrest the free-fall in output growth. In addition, Singapore also saw it as an opportune time to upgrade its labour force for the next wave of regional growth. It implemented several training programmes and gave incentives to employers.

Banking and Financial Sector Measures

In the face of unanticipated and untoward global developments, the MAS's main objective was to keep the
Singapore money and credit markets functioning normally.
It ensured enough liquidity in the system to maintain market
confidence. It also made sure that the financial market
would not run short of U.S. dollars to meet any obligations
amid the global financial meltdown and set up a US$30
billion swap line with the U.S. Federal Reserve.

The policymakers of Singapore also came up with
several innovative measures to contain the contagion from
the outside. The government provided a guarantee on
bank deposits to restore depositors' confidence in local
banks. Moving in line with other central banks in the
region, Singapore took this step as a precaution to avoid
any erosion of banks' deposit base and consequently
ensured a level international playing field for Singapore
banks.

The SRI was necessary to maintain the credit flows
to worthy borrowers. As the collapse of Singapore exports
was partly attributable to severe disruption in trade
financing amid the banking turmoil, the SRI scheme
was expected to help exporters obtain loans and trade
insurance on the scale they needed. The scheme also
aimed to stimulate bank lending and ensure that viable
companies would continue to have access to credit to
sustain their operations. Indeed, as of December 2009,
the SRI has moved more than 14,000 loans worth about
SG$8 billion. More than 13,000 companies have benefited
from the scheme.

Monetary Policy Measures

Following the outbreak of the crisis in September 2008, the MAS took a gradualist approach to ease its monetary policy and cushion the rapidly decelerating economy. It took a stance of zero appreciation for the Singapore dollar and later shifted the NEER policy band downwards. In the absence of domestic inflationary pressures, the MAS had allowed the Singapore dollar to fall against the U.S. dollar in line with other regional currencies. This was mainly to raise confidence in the face of a worsening global outlook.

Fiscal Policy Measures

Singapore's fiscal policy measures were aggressive and appropriate. As the government realized the severity of the economic downturn, it unveiled a SG$20.5 billion "Resilience Package" for the FY2009 budget. The budget had three broad objectives: (a) boosting employment and minimizing job dismissals, (b) reducing business costs, (c) strengthening economic infrastructure through accelerating development projects and providing more funds for skills development and training. While the first two objectives were mainly to ride out the current recession, the third objective was to strengthen the country's long-term competitiveness and emerge stronger after the crisis. The government also supported specific sectors such as the property market and assisted households to lessen the pain from the economic recession.

    The FY2009 budget preferred to fine-tune a few existing programmes rather than introduce extra spending plans. This helped to lessen the burden on the government's fiscal position. For instance, after the presentation of the 2009 budget, the government rolled out the Finance Graduate Immersion Programme (FGIP) to provide unemployed fresh graduates with job opportunities with Singapore-based financial institutions. The bulk of the funding was proposed to come from the Financial Sector Development Fund. Thus the cost of taking on graduates for financial institutions, research institutes, and university departments was quite minimal.

The fiscal policy package also included some significant measures that are worth noting. They were targeted at individuals and companies, with a short implementation period, and were designed to be of a temporary nature to prevent the measures from becoming a permanent drain on resources in the long-term. For example, under the JCS for one year, with employers receiving 12 per cent cash on the first SG$2500 of each month's wages for every employee, this was equivalent to a 9 percentage points CPF rate cut, and would definitely help companies to maintain their headcounts. Also, there was no strain on employees' pockets. Second, the personal income tax rebate allowed the government to give some flexibility to households during the downturn without locking down rates and crimping on further tax revenue potential. Third, measures such as WIS at the lower income, GST credits, and government hiring plans were targeted at and were expected to have a major impact on output. The measures reduced losses in income for individuals and gave households more confidence in economic recovery, thus slowing the pace of increasing precautionary savings.

Similarly, the government's direct consumption of goods and services has a higher economic multiplier. It brought forward infrastructure projects and announced rejuvenating plans for public housing estates that would remain positive for the construction sector.

In addition to taking care of the crisis, Singapore policies also balanced the country's long-term objectives. For example, by cutting corporate income tax to among the lowest in the world, the government sharpened Singapore's cost competitiveness and prepared the country for the upturn. Moreover, as Singapore was running a balanced budget for most of the years prior to the crisis, fiscal policy in Singapore tended to be financed from accumulated budget surpluses rather than from borrowing. This enhanced the impact of temporary measures as the government was unlikely to need to finance fiscal policy through higher future taxes. Neither would the government need to borrow to finance the deficit — therefore it would not draw on the credit in the market and crowd out private investments.

The unprecedented fiscal stimulus package was estimated to result in a large deficit for FY2009 of SG$8.7 billion, or 3.5 per cent of GDP, almost four times that of 2001. However, the direct cost-cutting measures have improved Singapore's competitiveness. As can be seen in Figure 4.3, the unit labour cost of the overall economy has come down significantly in the first three quarters of 2009. Likewise, the unit business cost of the manufacturing sector has fallen sharply over the same period of 2009.

FIGURE 4.3

Declining Unit Business Cost and Unit Labour Cost

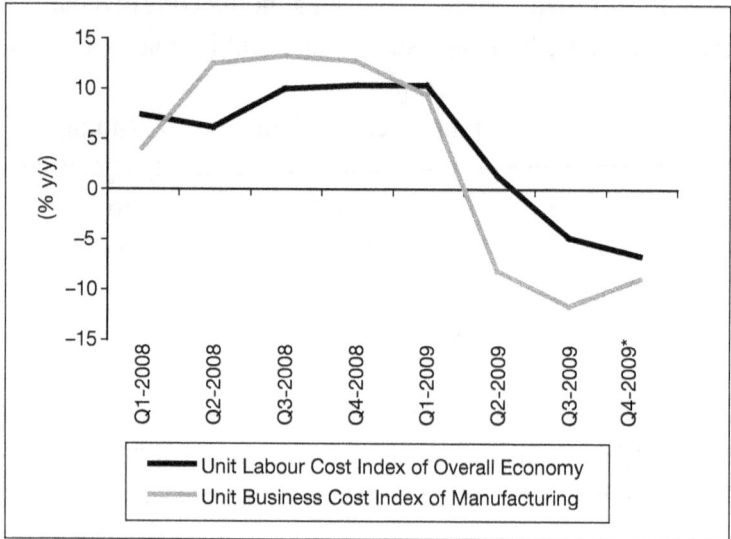

Note: * indicates predicted.
Source: Singapore Department of Statistics.

Since the announcement of the FY2009 budget in January 2009, the economy has been recovering strongly, registering a growth rate of 0.6 per cent and 4.0 per cent for the third and fourth quarters respectively. For the whole of 2009, Singapore experienced a contraction of 2.0 per cent compared to a predicted contraction of –4.0 to –6.0 during the release of advance estimates for Q2-2009 GDP on 14 July 2009. The labour market also rebounded sharply, as the unemployment rate dropped dramatically to 2.9 per cent in December 2009 from a high of 5.0 per cent earlier in the year.

Smaller FY2009 Revised Budget Deficit

As the Singapore economy emerged better than expected from the 2008 global economic crisis, the FY2009 budget balance turned out far better than initially projected. The income tax revenues exceeded projection on better than expected performance of both employment and incomes. Further, a strong recovery in the volume of transactions in the property market boosted stamp duty collections, which ended up SG$1.3 billion higher than initially estimated. As for the total expenditure, it fell moderately by 1.7 per cent. The decrease was largely attributed to lower manpower costs on reduced year-end bonuses and lower development expenditure on reduced construction costs and deferral of several development projects.

While the estimated basic deficit of SG$8.5 billion or 3.3 per cent of GDP for FY2009 was large, taking into account the NII contribution and the budgeted top-ups to endowment and trust funds, the Ministry of Finance (MOF) estimate a lower overall budget deficit of SG$2.9 billion (or 1.1 per cent of GDP) for FY2009 (Table 4.2). This is in comparison with the SG$8.7 billion (or 3.5 per cent of GDP) deficit budgeted a year ago.

Given the revised FY2009 budget numbers, the MOF assessed the macroeconomic impact of the 2009 fiscal policy. This was done using fiscal impulse, which measures whether the government's fiscal policy decisions during a given period of time are adding to, or subtracting from, aggregate demand pressures in the economy. According to the MOF, the fiscal impulse for 2009 is expected to be smaller than estimated at the start of FY2009. For the

TABLE 4.2

Revised Fiscal Position in FY2009
(as of 22nd February 2010)

	Revised FY2009 (in SG$ billion)	*% change compared to estimated*
Operating Revenue	38.6	15.4
Total Expenditure	42.9	−1.7
Primary Surplus/Deficit	−4.3	—
Special Transfers	5.6	−9.0
Basic Surplus/Deficit	−8.5	—
Net Investment Income	7.0	−8.3
Overall Budget Surplus/Deficit	2.9	—

Note: "−" indicates deficit.
Source: Ministry of Finance, Singapore.

whole of 2009, as Singapore's economy performed better than expected at the beginning of the year, the higher-than expected income tax and stamp duty collections moderated the fiscal impulse expected from the Resilience Package (Figure 4.4).

The MOF further measured the appropriateness of the fiscal impulse, which is often assessed against the prevailing state of the economy. This is done by looking at the output gap, which is defined as the difference between the actual output (GDP) of an economy and the output that the economy would be at under full capacity or maximum efficiency. According to MOF, the smaller fiscal impulse for 2009 is nearly appropriate given that the output gap was also less severe than predicted.

FIGURE 4.4
Almost Neutral Fiscal Impulse

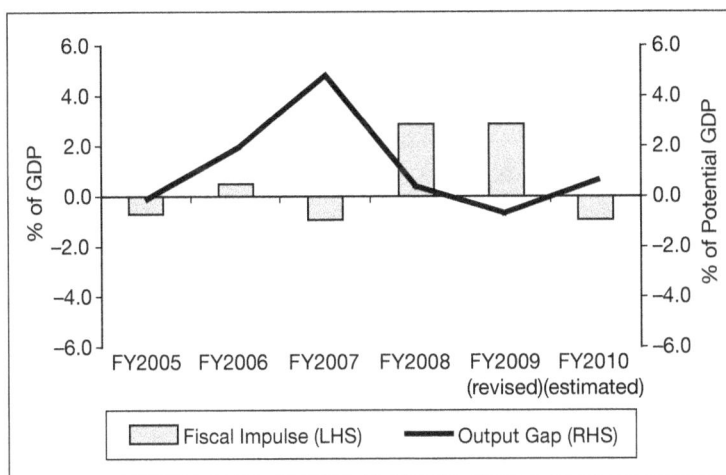

Source: Budget Highlights, Financial Year 2010, Ministry of Finance, Singapore.

Summing up

The Singapore Government and the MAS responded to the challenges strongly and adequately. The government realized the seriousness of the problem and decided to use the full array of fiscal measures to mitigate the effects of the crisis. It focused on the employability of people and helped corporates to drive down cost and preserve employees. The economic downturn also became an opportunity for exploring new growth strategies and investments in skills development, training, and infrastructure to improve competitiveness in the longer term.

The MAS shifted its FX policy stance from monetary tightening to monetary easing in response to easing inflationary pressure and falling output engendered by the global crisis. The central bank's policy response was aimed at protecting the economy and its financial sector against any erosion of confidence. It maintained a comfortable level of Singapore dollar and U.S. dollar liquidity throughout the period of high uncertainty.

The 2009 budget introduced a Resilience Package to help cushion businesses and households from the impact of the economic downturn. The measures included tax exemption/rebate schemes and help for businesses to preserve jobs, enhance cashflow, and invest in infrastructure for the long-term.

Although all these policy actions were unable to forestall a recession, they mitigated the impact and averted an even sharper and prolonged downturn. Indeed, Singapore registered a positive rate of economic growth in the last two quarters of 2009 as the policies were implemented in a timely and effective manner, thus helping the city state to counter the negative fallout of the global slowdown.

Notes

1. As some of the expenditures in the FY2009 budget had been front-loaded to the first quarter of 2009, it was paid out of the FY2008 budget, raising the budget deficit much higher compared to that estimated at the start of FY2008.

5
Singapore's Economic Perspective and Future Policy Directions

Being a small and open economy, Singapore is susceptible to external shocks, but by the same measure, the city state tends to bounce back faster and stronger than many other regional economies. Thus, following the global economic recovery, Singapore also catapulted itself out of recession in the third quarter of 2009. The economy expanded by 0.6 per cent, the first expansion after three straight quarters of contraction. The growth was driven by expansion in the electronics manufacturing sector and improvements in the trade-related and tourism sectors on the back of a gradual stabilization in global economic conditions.

But this fast turnaround may not be without hiccups. Weak household balance sheets and persistently high unemployment, especially in the United States, might weigh down consumer demand in Singapore's key export markets. Although external demand will continue to grow, it will be at a sluggish pace. Growth momentum in the second half of 2010 may also slow down as the effects of global fiscal stimulus measures and inventory restocking wane. The city state may experience uneven recovery across sectors. According to the Ministry of Trade and Industry of Singapore, the economy is expected to grow by 4.5–6.5 per cent in 2010, after shrinking by 2.0 per cent in 2009.

World Economic Outlook

The global economic recovery seems to be well under way. Businesses and consumers are slowly realizing that worst-case scenarios are almost over and are adjusting their consumption, investment, and hiring behaviour according to a more benign economic behaviour. Most importantly, businesses are no longer cutting on their inventories. The advanced economies, which were hit particularly hard by the financial crises and the collapse in world trade, are showing signs of stabilization, driven mainly by an unprecedented public policy response. The rebound in emerging economies is being led by a resurgence of Asia, fuelled by policy stimulus and a turn in the global destocking activities. This was also reflected in the financial markets as investors' risk aversion declined, portfolio flows recovered, and stock prices rallied. For example, from its trough in March 2009 to the end of December 2009, the S&P 500, the DJ Euro Stoxx 50, and the MSCI Emerging Market rose 60 per cent, 65 per cent, and 108 per cent respectively. But the pace of recovery both in economic activities and the financial market is still very nascent and remains far below the pre-crisis level.

The private sector in many advanced economies is still over-stretched. U.S. households remain highly indebted and household balance-sheet problems remain important in the

United Kingdom, Spain, and Ireland. As these imbalances may come to the fore only by late 2010, there could be a slowdown in the United States and some other advanced economies in early 2011. However, this would entail only a softening of growth rather than a renewed widespread GDP deceleration.

That said, according to the forecast released by the IMF in January 2010 (Table 5.1):

- The world economy has been estimated to contract by 0.8 per cent in 2009, far below the 4.1 per cent growth rate achieved during 2007–8, prior to the crisis. Global activity is likely to expand by about 3.9 per cent in 2010 and another 4.3 per cent in 2011.

- As regards the advanced economies, output contracted by 3.2 per cent in 2009 (as against an expansion of 0.5 per cent in 2008) on households' loss of confidence in the real and the financial economy. Annual growth is projected to recover gradually in 2010 and 2011 to about 2.1 per cent and 2.4 per cent respectively, with unemployment continuing to rise for 2010.

- The growth rates in the emerging and developing economies were forecast to reach around 6.1 per cent in 2010–11, up from 2.1 per cent in 2009. While China's growth is projected to rise from 8.7 per cent in 2009 to 9.8 per cent in 2010–11, growth in India is placed at 7.8 per cent for 2010 (vis-à-vis 5.6 per cent in 2009) by the IMF. A stronger economic framework and appropriate policy response would help most of these economies to cushion imported shocks and re-attract capital flows quickly.

TABLE 5.1

World Economic Outlook Projections

	2008	*2009*	*2010*	*2011*
World Output	3.0	−0.8	3.9	4.3
Advanced Economies	0.5	−3.2	2.1	2.4
United States	0.4	−2.5	2.7	2.4
Euro area	0.6	−3.9	1.0	1.6
United Kingdom	0.5	−4.8	1.3	2.7
Japan	−1.2	−5.3	1.7	2.2
Emerging Economies	6.1	2.1	6.0	6.3
Developing Asia	7.9	6.5	8.4	8.4
China	9.6	8.7	10.0	9.7
India	7.3	5.6	7.7	7.8
ASEAN-5[1]	4.7	1.3	4.7	5.3
World Trade Volume	2.8	−12.3	5.8	6.3
(goods and services)				
Consumer Prices				
Advanced Economies	3.4	0.1	1.3	1.5
Emerging Economies	9.2	5.2	6.2	4.6

[1] Indonesia, Malaysia, Philippines, Thailand, and Vietnam.
Source: IMF, *World Economic Outlook Update*, January 2010.

- Regarding the world trade outlook, the IMF estimates that it is expected to grow by 5.8 per cent in 2010 and subsequently by 6.3 per cent in 2011. This is against a sharp contraction of 12.3 per cent in 2009.

Despite the positive outlook, there continue to be risks surrounding the global economic environment. Governments around the world are expected to reduce their fiscal stimulus packages and this may have implications for the domestic economy. Central banks are likely to raise the key interest rates or go for other tightening measures in anticipation of rising inflationary pressure. Lastly, in the long-term, the post-crisis global economy is likely to be very different from the past. A return to the heady growth rates based on excessive credit expansion seen before the crisis is highly unlikely (Table 5.2).

The new global average growth rate is likely to be lower, weighed down by slower growth in the advanced economies because of the balance sheet problems of households, banks, and the government. Emerging markets, on the other hand, will see a more rapid recovery and expansion. China may try to move up the production value chain and India may restructure its manufacturing sector for more efficiency. This will not only change the competitive landscape in the global economy but will also result in large capital flows to emerging markets with important implications for the exchange rate, domestic liquidity, and inflation. These developments could shift the centre of economic gravity from the advanced countries to the Asian region. But much will depend on policies implemented to manage the transition process.

TABLE 5.2
Long-term World GDP Outlook

	2004–6	*2007–11*	*2012–15*
World	4.8	3.0	4.3
Advanced Economies	3.0	0.9	2.9
Emerging and Developing Economies	7.5	5.7	6.7

Source: EIU, IMF WEO Database, author's estimates.

As the crisis ebbs, there will be critical issues that would need to be tackled by the policymakers. First, with buoyant recovery in emerging Asia, the oil price is bound to rise strongly. This will translate into higher costs that would squeeze corporate profits. Asian economies are particularly sensitive to commodity inflation as both the weight of food and energy account for a significant proportion of the CPI basket at between 33 per cent and 50 per cent. Second, financial regulators will shift their focus from individual instruments and institutions to encompass the macro-prudential dimension. This will imply larger capital buffers and new limits on risk taking.

Most importantly, in the post-crisis era, policymakers are going to face a major challenge to rebalance the global economy. Advanced economies that experienced asset price busts will need to switch resources to externally driven growth. They will need to consolidate their fiscal position after the crisis and raise private savings. On the other hand, economies such as those in Asia that previously relied on export-led growth will need to gradually switch to domestically-driven growth through the optimal use of policy mix. In the case of Asia, its relatively strong banking sector, high national savings (25–50 per cent of GDP) as well as huge foreign exchange reserves (US$4 trillion) should provide support to aggregate demand. Fiscal resources could be directed to strengthening social safety nets to reduce households' precautionary savings. Asia's savings need to be ploughed back to the region, especially for the financing of socio-economic and infrastructure spending. This may require deepening of regional bond and capital markets to facilitate the mobilization of Asia's high level of savings to support spending in the region. As part of the re-balancing effort, many Asian countries may have to increase currency flexibility.

All this implies that rebalancing global growth and an increase in emerging market domestic demand does not mean that emerging economies will become inward looking and reduce trade and financial linkages. Rather, it means reviving domestic demand and removing bottlenecks to domestic spending. It also means boosting intra-regional trade through structural reforms and boosting rates of return for domestic assets.

Indeed, during 2012–15, world trade is expected to grow by an annual average rate of 6.0 per cent (vis-à-vis 1.2 per cent in 2008–11), driven by faster growth in developing countries as they continue with their process of integration. As we observe in Asia, bilateral and regional level trade liberalization has made a lot of progress in the last few years. Early 2010 saw ASEAN realizing its free trade agreements (FTAs) with China and South Korea, as well as the entry into force of the ASEAN-Australia–New Zealand FTA and the ASEAN-India Trade in Goods Agreement. India concluded an FTA with South Korea in July 2009 and South Korea also signed an agreement with the European Union in October. A host of further FTAs, including preparations for talks with the United States and ASEAN, and other arrangements to deepen economic ties (including through FDI and trade in services) are in the pipeline.

Singapore's Economic Outlook

"V-shaped" Recovery

The Singapore economy rebounded strongly from a trough of 9.5 per cent contraction in Q1-2009 to a positive growth of 4.0 per cent in the final quarter of 2009. This is on the back of a sharp recovery in exports and the manufacturing sector. The city state's exports grew by 4.9 per cent in the fourth quarter of 2009, after four consecutive periods of double-digit declines. In particular, NODX to China, Taiwan, and Hong Kong have shown the strongest recovery following the sharp decline during the crisis. On the other hand, Singapore's NODX to the G-3 economies fell the sharpest in the recession, and by the end of 2009 were still around 23 per cent below the level in the first quarter of 2008. This reflects the relatively weak recovery in G-3 final demand, as tight labour and credit markets weighed on consumer spending and firm investment (Figure 5.1).

The surge in the manufacturing sector was primarily driven by a pickup in production of biomedical manufacturing in the second and third quarter of 2009. The other main component of the manufacturing sector — electronics — surged 27 per cent in the fourth quarter of 2009 after contracting sharply in the first half of the year.

The services sector recovered gradually with tourism and the trade-related sectors improving on the back of recovery in global trade flows and international travel. Visitor arrivals recovered strongly in the second half of 2009 due to better consumer and investor sentiments and various initiatives like the Building on Opportunities to Strengthen Tourism (BOOST)[1] implemented by the

FIGURE 5.1
Singapore's NODX to Selected Regions

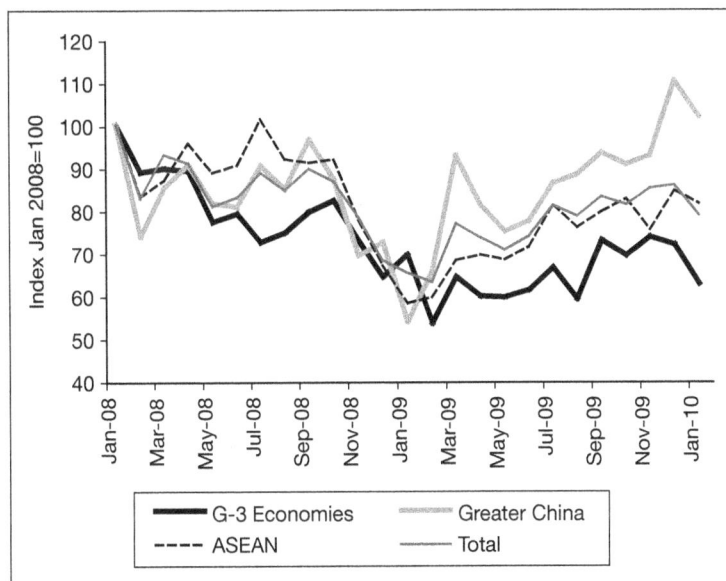

Note: ASEAN comprises Malaysia, Indonesia, Thailand.
Source: CEIC Database, author's calculation.

Singapore Tourism Board. Moreover, as the U.S. and European markets contribute just 18 per cent of visitor arrivals to Singapore compared to more than 45 per cent of visitor arrivals from ASEAN (Indonesia, Malaysia, Vietnam, the Philippines, and Thailand) and China, a turnaround in Asian economies had a profound impact on the sector. As for the construction sector, it showed a third straight year of double-digit expansion of 16 per cent. While construction demand fell sharply during the first half of 2009, there was a noticeable pickup in the second half of 2009, particularly in the level of public sector construction demand, which contributed 64 per cent to the overall demand in 2009.

With Singapore's economy bottoming out, the unemployment rate, after rising to 3.4 per cent in September 2009, improved significantly to 2.1 per cent in December 2009. With a slew of government policies — skills programme for upgrading and resilience, professional skills programme, and job credit — the impact of the crisis on the labour market seems to be less severe than initially feared. Continuing with this trend, the overall unemployment rate stabilized around 3.0 per cent in 2009 and is expected to remain there in 2010.

The Economy in 2010–11 and Beyond

Singapore's economic outlook will be heavily dependent on external developments. GDP growth in Singapore's major export markets is expected to improve in 2010–11, while Asian growth is set for rapid expansion. In line with the forecast for an improvement in the global economy, MTI has projected 2010 Singapore GDP to grow between 4.5 and 6.5 per cent.

In 2010 and early 2011, the growth momentum of Singapore is expected to taper off as much will weigh on the external factors. This can already be seen in the Q4-2009 quarter-on-quarter GDP growth number of –2.8 per cent, as against a double-digit pace of growth in Q2-2009 and Q3-2009. However, this does not mean that the recovery is losing steam. It is only shifting towards a more sustainable pace of growth in the coming quarters.

In 2010–11, Singapore's net exports will be supported by stronger global economic growth, but there will be no return to the rates of export growth that prevailed before the 2008 global economic crisis, as demand is expected to recover only gradually in Singapore's main export markets. Imports will also pick up in the next two years, reflecting stronger domestic demand and an increase in demand for inputs for the export-oriented manufacturing sector.

With gradual resumption of trade flows (Figure 5.2), the manufacturing sector is likely to expand moderately. The main driver of growth in the manufacturing sector, i.e. pharmaceuticals, might be volatile and may not show the

FIGURE 5.2

Exports Recovering for Most of the Markets

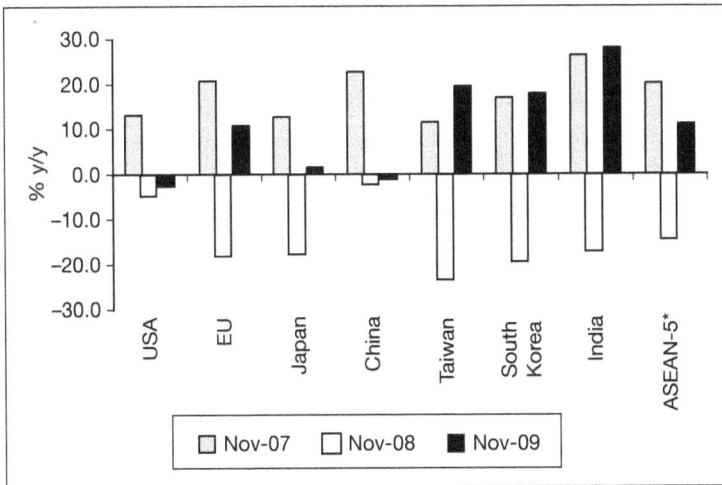

Note: *ASEAN-5 comprises Indonesia, Malaysia, the Philippines, Thailand, and Vietnam.
Source: CEIC Database, author's Calculation.

same high rates of growth seen in 2009. This is mainly because the strong growth in the pharmaceutical industry evident in 2009 was more due to H1NI flu, and as the impact of the flu wears off the global demand for drugs may dissipate. However, this will be compensated by improvement in the electronics industry as global recovery is expected to increase demand for electronic products. The construction sub-sector should continue to benefit from government proposals to develop infrastructure (new MRT lines) as well as rejuvenating some housing estates. The growth of the sector will also be driven by a number of large developments, including two integrated resorts (IRs) — Marina Bay Sands, which features a 2,500-room hotel, casino, and theatre; and Resorts World at Sentosa, which comprises six hotels with a total of 1,800 rooms, a casino, and an entertainment complex, Universal Studios Singapore.

Financial services will be buoyed by the booming property market and better investor sentiments. The global recovery will bring in strong consumer and business spending in overseas travel. As this will give rise to a steady flow of tourists, the two IRs will definitely give an uplift to tourism related sectors — retail and hotels. Finally, the resumption in global trade flows will surely bolster the growth in the wholesale trade and transport services segment. Thus, with a modest rebound in economic activities, the Singapore economy is likely to grow by 5.5 to 6.5 per cent in 2010–11.

While the chance of a *W*-shaped "double-dip" recession is small in the absence of further financial shocks, there remains a downside risk of premature exit from the loose fiscal and monetary policies pursued by countries around the world. The outlook for private final demand remains cautious, as weak labour markets in the United States and other advanced economies may constrain consumer and firm spending in these economies. In addition, there are concerns over rising oil prices which could fuel inflationary expectations and undermine a rebound in economic activity.

For the longer term (2012–15), with a change in global dynamics, Singapore may not experience the high economic growth rate of 7–8 per cent as in the past. The after-effects (such as fiscal pressures in some European and developing economies) of the financial and economic crisis are likely to weigh on the recovery. The country is likely to undergo a major economic restructuring and will probably move towards an innovation-led growth model. As the crisis brought forth the flaws of an export-led growth strategy, the Singapore Government will implement measures to increase domestic consumption. It will look for ways to strengthen new sources of growth such as education, healthcare, and tourism. Nevertheless, external demand will continue to be one of the key factors for the Singapore economy, and as global economic recovery goes on a more firm footing, private consumption and investment in the developed economies is likely to support the growth momentum of the city state's economy.

Future Policy Directions

In the short term the policy agenda will remain focused on supporting economic recovery. This is because, even though global growth is key to Singapore, the developed economies like the United States and the European Union — the largest export markets for Singapore — will need the necessary time and adjustments to overcome the impact of the crisis and this will continue to exert a drag on their economic activities. Over the next five years the government is expected to implement the recommend-ations of the ESC, a group the Prime Minister had set up in May 2009 to find ways to ensure Singapore's continued prosperity.

Fiscal Policy

Fiscal policy has always played a significant role in Singapore's economic downturn — the Asian crisis in 1997–98, the bursting of the tech-bubble in 2001, and the impact of SARS in 2009. In the current recession, with a lot of uncertainty about the depth and duration, fiscal policy again played a very important role. The policymakers see it as an important tool to cushion the impact of the crisis and lessen the pain of the vulnerable groups. Singapore is also in a position to use expansionary fiscal policies as counter-cyclical measures. It has healthy public finance and large fiscal reserves. This is further strengthened with the implementation of a constitutional amendment to the spending framework that allows the government to tap a larger share of the returns each year from the fiscal reserves invested by the country's two sovereign wealth funds, GIC and Temasek Holdings.

Singapore will continue with its expansionary fiscal measures, given the downside risk and the "uncertain" nature of the 2008 economic slowdown. However, the government is likely to scale it back eventually. For example, in the FY2010 budget, while the Jobs Credit Scheme has been continued for the first six months of 2010, the rates have been reduced to 6 per cent in the first quarter, and 3 per cent in the second quarter, compared to 12 per cent in 2009. The SRI will be phased out gradually over 2010 as well, with reductions in loan quantum limits and a lower share of lending risk borne by the government, before being fully withdrawn by the end of January 2011. In the next few years the government will ensure more fiscal discipline as the economy gradually recovers from the downturn. This is again evident in the FY2010 budget, which puts heavy emphasis on positioning Singapore for the next phase of growth, and projected an overall deficit of 1.1 per cent of GDP on higher revenues from taxes and fees.

In case of any major negative events later in 2010 or early 2011 such as dismal performance by advanced economies or a "double-dip" scenario, the government is willing to introduce off-budgetary measures if needed. This is to help allay fears and discourage precautionary saving motives of corporates and households, which in turn would safeguard the effectiveness of the fiscal measures already introduced.

The nature of the 2008 downturn and a constant sense of uncertainty also suggest a diversified stimulus package for both revenue and expenditure measures in the future. For Singapore, cash handouts are not effective in driving up domestic demand as a high proportion of such provisions would translate into higher imports.

Hence, measures to support household disposable income include tax incentives, a one-off personal income tax rebate, and targeted cash transfers. The government will continue with its emphasis on saving jobs and re-skilling through intensive training programmes. The policymakers in Singapore are also going to encourage the business sector, especially the SMEs, and incentives will be given in the form of credit programmes, credit guarantees, and trade finance. Significant allocations will also be made for public investment programmes to improve the physical and social infrastructure.

Monetary Policy

Due to the severity of the 2008 crisis, the MAS eased its monetary policy twice. First it moved the SG$ NEER to a neutral zero per cent appreciation stance in October 2008, then it re-centred the policy band downwards in April 2009. Since then the economy has been on its way to recovery, though amid uncertainty. This is also reflected in the SG$ NEER, which is about 1.7 per cent higher compared to the low in January 2009. Most of the second half of 2009, the SG$ NEER moved above the midpoint of the policy band. With economic activities picking up in 2010–11, the SG$ NEER will continue to stay at the stronger half of the policy band.

However, the MAS will refrain from any major moves in the short-run. There are still concerns about the medium-term growth outlook and slack in the labour market for the next few quarters. These will keep domestic price pressure subdued, except for property prices, which may move up fast on better market sentiments. The MAS will also keep a close watch on the U.S. Federal Reserve and other central banks in the region. Moreover, while the economy may post high year-on-year growth on an extreme low base in 2009, sequential growth for the coming quarters will average around 4–5 per cent q/q saar. That said, the MAS is likely to move back to its earlier policy stance of appreciation and shift the policy band upwards through the course of 2010. During this time, inflationary pressure is expected to firmly build up on more quality growth and low base effect.

Other Policies

Although Singapore has strong economic fundamentals, the 2008 crisis raised several questions regarding a sustainable healthy economic growth in future. This is especially in the light of change needed in the global demand pattern. The financial crisis highlighted the fact that many economies like developing Asia that have followed export-led growth strategies and have run current account surpluses in the past will have to encourage policies to support domestic demand (investment in most countries) and reduce reliance on export. On the other hand, economies like the United States and the United Kingdom that have run current account deficits must be encouraged to foster expanded savings. There is already some evidence of the needed change taking place in the United States. Private savings have risen and the U.S. current account deficit has fallen from more than 6.5 per cent of the GDP in late 2005 to about 3 per cent of the GDP in late 2009.

Moreover, economic growth in China and India are likely to surge in the coming years. According to IMF data, while China is expected to grow by more than 9.0 per cent, economic growth for India will almost touch 8.0 per cent in the next few years to 2015. Other than quantity, these countries may also shift their strategy to quality driven growth. In that case, these countries may become more competitive in areas that Singapore currently focuses on. In addition, the city state may experience higher vulnerability as oil prices move up and emerging economies' currencies appreciate on weaker U.S. dollar sentiments and better economic prospects.

To accommodate this shift on the global demand model and strong emergence of Asia led by China and India, Singapore must restructure the supply side of the economy and must prepare itself to take advantage of the emerging opportunities during the economic recovery.

Raise Labour Productivity

Singapore's labour productivity has been falling over the last few years. It had dropped from −0.4 per cent in 2007 to −6.9 in Q2-2008 and further to −14.6 per cent in the first three months of 2009 (Figure 5.3). This implies that labour productivity has already been declining, even during the period of normal economic growth. Although the declining productivity reversed during the downturn (−0.6 per cent in Q3-2009) on reduction of headcounts in firms, improving the productivity of the labour force is critical to strengthen the recovery of the economy.

FIGURE 5.3
Labour Productivity by Industry

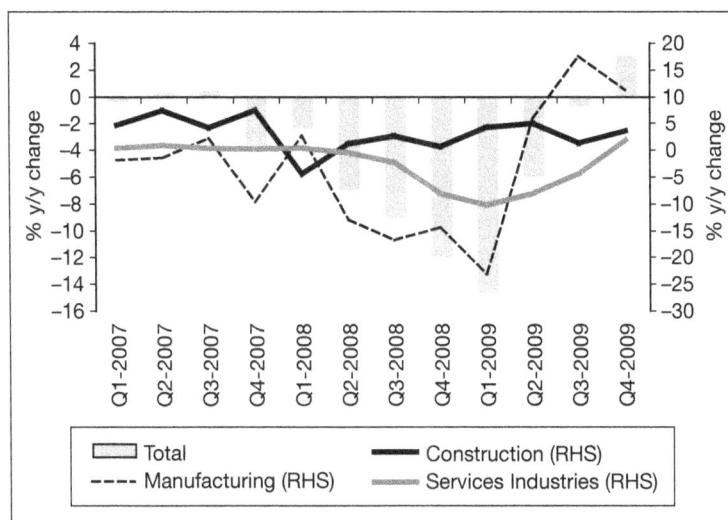

Source: *Economic Survey of Singapore* (various issues), MTI, Singapore.

To overcome this issue, on 1 February 2010, the ESC came up with wide-ranging recommendations, including limiting growth in the number of foreign workers, freeing up land for development, and increasing productivity growth by improving labour skills and relying more heavily on technology and innovation (Box 5.1). The committee also identified three broad priorities: boosting skills in every sector, deepening the corporate sector's capabilities, and making Singapore a "distinctive global city and endearing home". The main tangible target is that of raising the rate of productivity growth to 2–3 per cent a year over the

BOX 5.1

Key Proposals of the Economic Strategies Committee

Target: 2–3 per cent annual productivity growth over ten years to drive GDP growth of 3–5 per cent and higher incomes.

Top Priorities: Boost skills in every job; Deepen corporate capabilities; Be a distinctive global city and endearing home.

Highlights:

- Form high-level national council to lead productivity drive and expand continuing worker training.
- Set up National Productivity Fund to provide grants for industry initiatives.
- Raise foreign worker levy progressively.
- Maintain manufacturing at 20–25 per cent of economy for high-value, complex activities.
- Build Singapore as a global-Asia hub for services and as a consumer business centre.
- Position Singapore as a premier hub for MNCs and global and Asian mid-size firms.
- Double the number of Singapore firms with revenues over SG$100 million to 1,000 by 2020.
- Fund new capital for SMEs to expand overseas, through public-private co-investments.
- Raise R&D spending to 3.5 per cent of GDP by 2015.
- Diversify energy sources; consider even the nuclear option.
- Plan ahead for a new waterfront city at Tanjong Pagar in twenty years' time.
- Create new underground spaces and projects.
- Rejuvenate mature industrial estates; identify new business sites.
- Attract and nurture diverse talents.

Source: ESC Report.

next decade and ensuring that annual real GDP growth averages 3–5 per cent.

In terms of boosting skills, the committee recommended the establishment of a high-level national council to oversee efforts to increase productivity and expand a nationwide Continuing Education and Training (CET) system. It also advised that levies on foreign workers be progressively raised so as to manage companies' dependence on imported labour. The preference for a price mechanism to control the number of foreign workers, rather than a quota system, reflects the idea of providing a greater degree of flexibility to companies.

The committee's recommendations on deepening corporate capabilities were threefold: to increase expenditure on research and development (R&D) to around 3.5 per cent of GDP in five years' time, from 3 per cent currently; to establish a specialized financial institution, similar to an export-import bank, to enable local firms to take advantage of opportunities in Asia; and to promote stronger alliances between large and small businesses. In terms of making Singapore a "global city", the committee recommended two broad strategies. First, it called for the development of "creative and arts clusters" and for efforts to make the city state a centre for "thought and practice leadership" in its main areas of specialization. Second, the committee recommended the development of physical infrastructure that will provide residents with the highest quality of life in Asia. This would require the rejuvenation of mature government-built HDB properties, as well as the development of "eco-towns" and new models for resource-efficient industrial clusters (Appendix III).

All this implies that Singapore is almost ready to shift to innovation and skill-led growth in its next phase of economic development. It is now the turn of the businesses to look at emerging sectors and seek new ways to produce higher value-added outputs. In the *Singapore Competitiveness Report 2009*, it was reported that re-exports (defined as "goods that were exported without undergoing any transformation except repacking, sorting, grading, marking, and similar activities") have made up an increasing proportion of all exports from Singapore since 1990. This is certainly a worrying trend given that the Singapore Government has sought to remake Singapore as a value-added, high-tech growth hub.

The government strongly supported this transformation through the FY2010 budget, which focused on raising productivity over the next five years and laid out concrete measures for a restructured advanced economy (Box 5.2). The key thrusts of the FY2010 budget were (a) growing incomes through skills and innovation, (b) growing globally competitive companies, and (c) including everyone in growth. In the words of Finance Minister Tharman Shanmugaratnam, "We are charting a new course for our economy, growing it by improving productivity. This will put us onto a virtuous cycle: building superior skills, quality jobs and higher incomes".

The 2010 budget addressed ways to increase productivity in the form of a Productivity and Innovation Credit (PIC), a tax allowance to defray acquisition costs, and a Workfare Training Scheme (Appendix IV). The PIC is a big tax perk — offering 250 per cent tax deduction — to spur business spending in a range of activities from

BOX 5.2
Singapore Budget – FY2010

Boosting Productivity

The government will commit SG$1.1 billion a year over the next five years to boost productivity. There will be continuing education for young Singaporeans, and further incentives for employers and low-wage workers to commit to training. Broader tax deductions for innovation, R&D, and the acquisition and registration of intellectual property. Greater incentives for private R&D.

Foreign Workers Levies

To be increased and phased in, starting this year, to encourage companies to rely less on lower-skilled foreign workers. As a first step, levy rates will be raised by between SG$10 and SG$30 a month for most work permit holders.

Encouraging Enterprise

One-off tax allowance, for five years, for M&A deals – to defray a portion of acquisition costs. Stamp duty waived on transfer of unlisted shares for M&A deals. These will cost the government SG$100 million a year. New incentives for angel investors; government to co-invest in SMEs.

Property Tax

The flat property tax rate has been replaced by a progressive property tax schedule for owner-occupied residential properties, with a higher rate for more expensive properties.

Personal Reliefs

Relief for wives who support their husbands and greater reliefs for those who have to look after their parents and grandparents, especially handicapped ones.

Source: Ministry of Finance, Singapore.

staff training to automation and research and development. On the labour aspect, SG$2.5 billion will be spent over the next five years on continuing education and training to raise skills and qualifications. This is also relevant for those workers who were retrenched during the crisis as they have to be updated on the latest labour market conditions.

A National Productivity Fund with a target size of SG$2 billion was created to provide grants for enterprises, with the construction sector a key beneficiary, receiving SG$250 million of the first SG$1 billion. A National Productivity and Continuing Education Council will be set up to institutionalize the productivity push.

To manage the size of the foreign workforce, the FY2010 budget proposed to raise levy rates over the next three years. Levy rates on work permit holders will be raised by between SG$10 and SG$30 starting 1 July 2010, and the total increase in levy rates will be SG$100 over the three years of 2010–12 per worker in the manufacturing and services sector. This may hurt labour-intensive companies in Singapore in the short-term, but as companies adapt by restructuring, this should be beneficial in the long run. Raising levy rates is also a more flexible tool compared to imposing quotas on foreign workers.

Given this, the budgeted FY2010 position is a basic deficit of SG$7.2 billion (or 2.6 per cent of GDP). After factoring in the top-ups to endowment and trust funds, and net investment income (NII) of SG$7.8 billion, the estimated out-turn for FY2010 is an overall deficit of SG$3.0 billion (1.1 per cent of GDP) (Table 5.3).

TABLE 5.3
Fiscal Position in FY2010

	Operating Revenue	Total Expenditure	Primary Surplus/ Deficit	Less Special Transfer	Basic Surplus/ (Deficit)	Add NII	Overall Budget Surplus/Deficit
Estimated FY2010 (SG$ billion)	40.7	46.4	−5.6	5.2	−7.2	7.8	−2.96

Note: "−" implies deficit.
Source: Ministry of Finance, Singapore.

Develop Strong SMEs

SMEs (employing less than 200 workers) are an important part of the Singapore economy. They make up about 90 per cent of enterprises and account for more than 10 per cent in overall GDP. According to the EDB, Singapore SMEs accounted for nearly 42 per cent of employment in 2006 but contributed only 24 per cent of the total manufacturing employment. This indicates that Singapore SMEs play a limited role in manufacturing as the sector is mainly dominated by multinational corporations (MNCs) and government-linked companies. However, SMEs in Singapore are important as they not only create new jobs but also provide linkages for larger firms.

Thus, the downturn might give a good opportunity to develop strong SMEs in Singapore. The ESC in its report proposed SG$1.5 billion to help home-grown firms in terms of funding and finding new markets. The other suggestions to make Singapore's SMEs globally competitive include developing an export-import (Exim) bank, which would offer risk insurance for trade-finance and overseas investments, and would ease financing difficulties that firms face when trying to expand abroad, especially the emerging market economies.

As the 2010 budget charted a new course of growth based on skills, innovation, and productivity, it provided SMEs with broad-based initiatives, all aimed at helping them capture growth opportunities both in and outside the country. To make innovation pervasive, the budget introduced a PIC to target a range of activities, benefiting more companies. In addition to R&D, it also covered investment in new product and industrial designs, acquisition of intellectual property rights, registration of intellectual property rights, investment in automation through technology or software, and training of employees. The budget also realized that MNCs are valuable partners of the SMEs and collaboration with MNCs can help SMEs develop new and cutting-edge competencies. To this end, a new programme called Partnerships for Capability Transformation (PACT) has been introduced to help SMEs develop the competencies needed to meet stringent manufacturing quality and certification requirements. A sum of SG$250 million has been set aside to help companies pay for such expenses.

These policies to raise productivity and innovation capabilities of SMEs will play an important role in sustaining employment and competitiveness of the economy. The skill upgrading programme is likely to help employees acquire special management skills as investing in training by SMEs is sometimes a risky intangible investment. By establishing the Exim bank, SMEs would also be encouraged to gain access to new markets, particularly in light of a number of bilateral free trade agreements that Singapore is party to. Hence, this is the time for SMEs to take advantage of the proposed programmes by the policymakers and propel themselves into a position to seize opportunities offered by a rising Asia.

Engaging with Asia — Major External Policies

ASEAN Economic Community: Singapore must take advantage of being a part of the larger AEC. The region is a growing market of 600 million people with a combined GDP of US$1.5 trillion. The AEC Blueprint, signed by the ASEAN leaders on 20 November 2007, aims to transform ASEAN into a single market and production base by 2015. With free movement of goods, services, investment, and skilled labour and freer flow of capital, the AEC will foster a pro-business environment, lower consumer prices, and boost productivity and prospects for sustainable development. The single market will provide economies of scale and will help to attract larger foreign direct investments. With the emergence of China and India as two global economic powers, the AEC will be in an ideal position to complement the new industrial structure that will emerge in Asia. As a stronger economic base helps to ride out global crises faster, Singapore must engage ASEAN more deeply in its future growth strategies.

Intra-Regional Trade: Singapore must give more importance to regional trade in Asia. This is in light of the proliferation of cross-border production networks in the region. The trade is generally dominated by intermediate products, like electronics products, which account for about 70 per cent of intra-Asian trade in parts and components for machinery and transport equipment, compared to a little over 30 per cent in NAFTA (North American Free Trade Agreement) signatory countries and Europe. Moreover, during 1980–2006, intra-regional trade as a share of East Asia's total trade increased from 37 per cent to 55 per cent (including Japan) or from 23 per cent to 46 per cent over the same period (excluding Japan). As per capita purchasing power rises in the region, Asian consumers will generate more demand for intra-Asian goods and services. Singapore also needs to raise the proportion of final goods in intra-regional trade, as well as exploit further opportunities in services trade. Hence as other western markets dry up and there is higher protectionism due to the economic crisis, Singapore must ride the storm with the emergence of a stronger Asia.

Exploring New Markets: As the export demand from Singapore's key markets flatten (the United States and Europe), it should look for new markets around the world. The country can continue with its export-led growth strategy, but only with a redirection of exports other than the G-3 economies. Regarding this, the city state has been vigorously signing FTAs beyond the region. Its FTA strategy has been pursued with twin goals. The first is to strengthen its economic linkages and gain a "first-mover" advantage vis-à-vis its major trading partners and remain globally competitive. The second goal, which is more relevant in light of the 2008 crisis, has been to enhance its market access to emerging market economies that have been equally committed to trade and investment liberalization. The country already has a network of eighteen regional and bilateral FTAs with twenty-four trading partners, promoting not only cross-border trade and investments but also encouraging research and development for the knowledge-based economy.

Summing Up

Since the second half of 2009, global economic conditions have started to improve. Singapore also emerged from its recession. To a large extent, the recovery is associated with the quick and counter-cyclical monetary and fiscal policies that were designed to limit the sharp fall in output and preserve employment to shore up confidence.

However, experts are still cautious on a smooth and sustainable recovery for the economy. There are huge debates on ways to withdraw the stimulus measures pursued by countries around the world. Any hasty removal of these packages may again jeopardize the nascent recovery of the global economy. In the case of Singapore, while high openness has made the economy more susceptible to global headwinds, it also enables the economy to pick up strongly when the global recovery gets under way. For 2010–11, domestic fiscal policy and external demand will be important factors contributing to Singapore's growth trajectory. The MTI expects the city state's economy to grow by 4.5 to 6.5 per cent in 2010. Thereafter, it is expected to grow between 3.0 to 5.0 per cent for the next five years.

The 2008 global crisis raised several important considerations regarding Singapore's growth model and economic competitiveness. This is also recognized by the Singapore policymakers, who are rapidly identifying new development models that can deliver sustained economic growth. They have realized that there are limits for manufacturing demand from the United States and Europe, and hence it is critical for the city state to engage deeply in ASEAN and Asia.

Since the crisis started, the government also focused on reviving the supply-side fundamentals of the economy. The ESC in February 2010 laid out a blueprint to reshape the economy with quality-driven growth. It aimed to double annual productivity gains to 2–3 per cent over a ten years span and put an emphasis on better skills in every job. Another key idea of the ESC's strategies centres on the need to moderate the rapid growth of foreign labour. It suggested the levy mechanism as the most flexible way to manage the number of workers, as it will allow the dynamic firms to seize business opportunities without being constrained by rigid quotas.

Being a follow-through of the ESC recommendations, the FY2010 budget focused on long-term supply-side economic development. It employed fiscal tools in several ways — promote economic growth through productivity and innovation, nurture a more dynamic corporate sector, and ensure that economic growth remains inclusive in nature. However, the budgetary measures alone may not achieve the government's ambitious goal of raising productivity growth. Businesses must also seek new ways to raise productivity by incrementally improving their existing activities.

All this implies that the government thinks the immediate crisis is over and Singapore must prepare itself to maximize growth capacity as the global economy resumes its upward growth trajectory. However, the government also remains alert to downside risks into the latter part of 2010 as Finance Minister Tharman Shanmugaratnam sounded a cautionary note on global economic prospects during his speech on the FY2010 budget.

Note

1. BOOST is a SG\$90 million initiative by the Singapore Tourism Board to help the tourism sector ride through the challenging times.

6
Lessons Learnt

The events of 2007–9 highlighted several lessons for the policymakers. This chapter focuses on six broad interrelated themes:

1. Decoupling theory a myth
2. Globalization adds vulnerability but also increases efficiency
3. Strong economic fundamentals give more room to handle the crisis
4. Market discipline is necessary
5. Stimulus packages need to be timely and carefully designed
6. Coordinated policy action helps in faster recovery

Decoupling Theory a Myth

Prior to the crisis, there were a lot of discussions on decoupling of emerging and developing economies from the West. In other words, it was believed that even if the advanced economies went into recession, Asia would be affected very marginally and would largely continue with its growth. However, during the economic crisis in a rapidly globalizing world, the decoupling theory has almost lost its credibility. The reduction in growth has not been limited to the advanced economies. The decline from the actual growth rate for 2007 to the growth rate estimated for 2009 is essentially identical for all four groups of countries: 6.3 percentage points for the world on average, 6.1 percentage points for the advanced economies, 6.6 percentage points for the emerging and developing economies, and 7.6 percentage points for those in the Western Hemisphere.

In the case of Singapore, which is a highly open economy, the transmission of the crisis took place through both trade and financial channels. Even though Singapore had very limited exposure to the toxic assets, the economy suffered the consequences of the recession that gripped the advanced economies of the world.

Globalization Adds Vulnerability but Also Increases Efficiency

Globalization of trade (merchandise and services), finance, and labour (demand for labour and flow of remittances) had tied countries together to a much greater extent than they had been earlier. Any crisis that affects a major country or group of countries in the global economy or financial system will have some adverse effects on all other countries. For the 2008 economic crisis, even though its genesis was in the U.S. system, it affected nations far away from the United States.

In the context of Singapore, its economy is one of the most open in the world. With a few exceptions, tariffs are zero, total merchandise trade is nearly four times GDP, and inflows of foreign direct investment are substantial. This high degree of openness leaves Singapore vulnerable to periodic external shocks. In addition, Singapore's role as a regional financial hub has increased its exposure to financial weaknesses among regional economies.

On the positive side, globalization has forced Singapore to improve overall economic management and increase efficiency. It compelled the city state to develop social and economic institutions through administrative, legislative, and legal reforms to remain attractive among regional economies. In this context, Singapore already strives to do the following:

1. Develop human capital as it is a prerequisite for successful globalization. The knowledge economy requires educated and skilled people.
2. Build up domestic savings and put them to productive use.
3. Maintain strong macro-economic fundamentals.
4. Establish good governance at all levels.
5. Run an effective regulatory authority as an important requirement of an open economy.

Thus, while globalization and a high degree of openness for Singapore implies increased vulnerability to external shocks, it also compels the city state to better economic management, which eventually enables it to adjust to external disturbances by increasing efficiency and competitiveness.

Strong Economic Fundamentals Give More Room to Handle the Crisis

In the face of a global crisis, a country will be better off if it has strong macro-economic fundamentals. This implies that the country's fiscal affairs are reasonably stable, the inflation rate is low, the internal and external debt position is sustainable, and foreign reserve are ample. All this will make the country better off and will give it room to respond to external shocks through the use of appropriate domestic policies.

Singapore has withstood the global crisis and has been almost on the path of recovery because of its strong economic fundamentals. With high current account surpluses, high savings rates, strong inflow of FDI, and negligible non-performing loans, Singapore was able to take timely and bold measures to counter the adverse shocks triggered by the crisis. In addition, due to sufficient accumulated foreign exchange reserves from the past, the Government of Singapore used them to fund two extraordinary measures, which were temporary in nature and would not build into longer-term government programmes. This was on the grounds of exceptional circumstances that the country faced during the crisis.

Singapore also has a good track record of prudent fiscal and monetary policies and this came out as a great asset during the dislocations. It helped reassure the stakeholders that the fiscal and monetary easing taken by the authorities to address short-term problems are less likely to endanger the future commitments to its long-term goals.

Market Discipline is Necessary

Singapore's financial system remained relatively resilient throughout the crisis. This was due to the robust regulatory framework and the rigorous supervisory approach followed by the MAS. It promoted transparency and market discipline in the financial system, which is expected to improve the quality of financial information available to the public and investors. To achieve this, the MAS required local banks to adopt public disclosures in addition to their financial statements. This will provide detailed information of their risk profile and financial strength. More recently, Singapore has committed to align fully with International Financial Reporting Standards by 2012.

In the area of prudential regulation, the MAS already requires local banks to meet minimum capital requirements which are higher than international standards, as well as liquidity and provisioning requirements which were not widely adopted internationally prior to the crisis, but are now regarded as necessary and appropriate. In December 2009, the Basel Committee on Banking Supervision released a package of proposals to strengthen global capital and liquidity regulations for consultation. These are targeted for adoption internationally by end-2012. Singapore's robust regulatory framework and the strong capital and liquidity positions of financial institutions mean that the country is well placed to meet new stringent international regulatory standards.

Finally, the crisis has led regulators in many countries to re-examine aspects of their approach regarding the sale and marketing of derivative structured products.

In Singapore, the MAS undertook a review of the regulatory regime governing the sale and marketing of unlisted investment products. In March 2009, the MAS published its policy consultation paper with proposals that covered issues such as promoting more effective disclosure, strengthening fair dealing in the sale and advisory process, introducing an enhanced regulatory regime for the sale of complex investment products, and enhancing the MAS's powers.

Thus, a number of prudential measures have been put in place over the past several years in order to maintain stability in the Singapore financial system, and these measures have contributed to domestic macroeconomic and financial stability in the times of fallout from the financial crisis.

Stimulus Packages Need to be Timely and Carefully Designed

Restoring consumer and business confidence is key to achieving financial stability and, eventually, growth recovery. This entails substantial support from the governments and the central banks. Governments have been addressing the 2008 recession through growth stimulus packages, while tax receipts were taking the brunt in the face of lower economic activity. However, these contributions from the government must be carefully designed so that they support the short-term needs of the domestic economy and do not leave any long-term implications for the fiscal structure of the country. The support packages must also be prompt as the longer it takes to effectively implement the measures, the more protracted would be the economic recession. Moreover, there could be more time for negative feedback from one sector to another, making the recession more pronounced.

In this case, Singapore's policy responses to the global financial and economic crisis have been timely and practical. Following the sudden eruption of the crisis in September 2008, the MAS took steps to ease its monetary policy to soften the blow from external headwinds. Later, other cost-cutting measures were introduced to strengthen Singapore's competitiveness. Realizing the severity of the crisis, the government preponed the budget announcement by one month to January 2009. The 2009 budget aimed at the supply side of the economy, more particularly on keeping jobs, as for Singapore the conventional fiscal and monetary policies to boost domestic demand are not very effective. In addition, Singapore took the opportunity of low global activity to position its economy for the next wave of global growth by investing in soft and hard infrastructure.

Coordinated Policy Action Helps in Faster Recovery

Since the onslaught of the global financial and economic crisis in 2008, many countries have unveiled various stimulus packages to bolster their weakening economies and fight the effects of a global slowdown. In November 2008, China and Germany proposed economic stimulus plans of US$586 billion and US$40 billion respectively; Canada proposed a plan worth about US$24 billion in

January 2009; France unveiled a US$34 billion plan in February 2009; the United States Senate and the House of Representatives reached a final deal on a US$789 billion economic stimulus bill in February 2009; and Singapore came up with a US$15 billion plan in January 2009.

While the primary focus of each stimulus package is to revive economic growth in their respective countries, they also had ramifications for other economies. This is especially because the nations are ever more dependent on each other in regard to export and investment growth, securities and property markets, and even consumer and investor confidence. This implies that the stimulus package and recovery plan of one country can eventually lead to relief and growth in another.

Thus, in an increasingly globalized world, where financial and economic woes can spread quickly, the policy response must be global, coordinated, and fast. Policy challenges need to be addressed at the country level, but the international community must act in a coordinated and supportive fashion to make each country's task easier.

On the whole, the broad lesson from the 2008 crisis is that globalization had tied countries together to a much greater extent than they had been two decades ago. This nature of the world economy makes financial or economic crises inevitable. Any crisis that affects a major country will have some effect on other countries. Thus, national economies need to have a strong economic framework and sustainable macroeconomic balances. The banking sector — core of any economy — has to be well capitalized and prudently regulated all the time. Apart from that, coordinated policies and efforts to improve quality of economic growth and the financial system are better ways of limiting the adverse impact during a crisis. In this regard, cooperation and commitment through the G-20 or any other international vehicle will remain essential.

APPENDIX I
MAS Monetary Policy
Statements

Date: 12 October 2009

Introduction

1. In April 2009, MAS re-centred the exchange rate policy band downwards to the prevailing level of the SG$NEER, while maintaining the zero per cent appreciation path which was adopted in October 2008. This decision was made against the backdrop of dissipating inflationary pressures and weak growth prospects for the Singapore economy in the midst of the global financial crisis.

2. Since the last policy review, the S$NEER (Figure 1) has fluctuated in the upper half of the policy band. This reflected the broad-based weakness in the US$ since the end of the first quarter, as well as strong capital inflows to the region. The domestic three-month interbank rate has remained at 0.69 per cent over the past six months, amidst low global interest rates.

Reproduced with the permission of the Monetary Authority of Singapore © 2008 and 2009 The Monetary Authority of Singapore.

FIGURE 1

Nominal Effective Exchange Rate (SG$NEER)

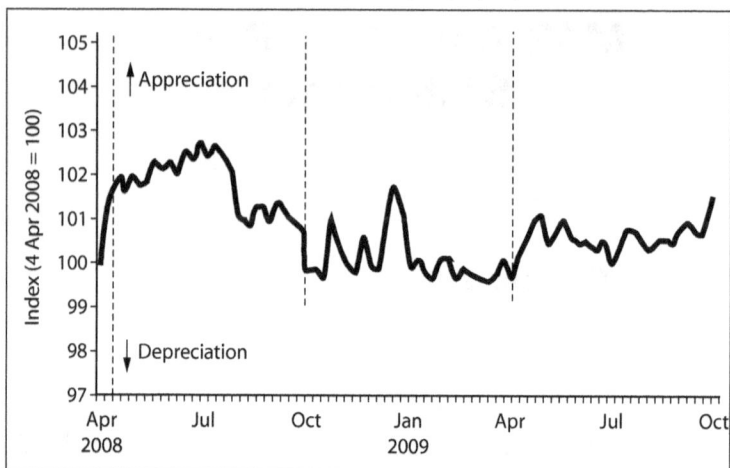

- - - - - indicates release of Monetary Policy Statement.

Outlook for 2009 and 2010

3.   Following the sharp contractions in Q4-2008 and Q1-
2009, the Singapore economy rebounded strongly by
22 per cent on a quarter-on-quarter seasonally adjusted
annualised (q-o-q SAAR) basis in Q2-2009. The
easing of global financial conditions and inventory
restocking had benefited the domestic financial market
and manufacturing activity. According to the Advance
Estimates released by the Ministry of Trade and
Industry today, Singapore's GDP expanded by a further
14.9 per cent q-o-q SAAR in Q3-2009, with a broad
range of industries across both the manufacturing and
services sectors registering positive growth. Reflecting

the better-than-expected outcome, Singapore's GDP growth forecast for 2009 has been revised upwards to between –2.5 per cent and –2 per cent, from –6 per cent to –4 per cent.[1]

4. Looking ahead, the economy is not expected to sustain the strong pace of expansion seen in Q2-Q3-2009. While prospects for the external economies have improved, final demand in Singapore's key export markets, including for IT products, has yet to recover decisively. Significant challenges remain in the transition to private sector–driven growth as governments prepare to exit from their expansionary policies. Household spending, particularly in the US, continues to be constrained by the weak labour market, sluggish income growth, and lower housing wealth. Businesses also remain cautious in their investment decisions. Against this backdrop, the Singapore economy is likely to settle at a more gradual pace of expansion. GDP growth in 2010 is expected to be slower than in previous post-recession periods.

5. The domestic CPI inflation rate averaged –0.5 per cent year-on-year over the period from April to August 2009. With the recovery in global oil prices, consumer prices picked up in July and August on a sequential basis, following two consecutive quarters of decline. Meanwhile, domestic cost pressures such as rentals and wages have come down significantly in response to the economic downturn. For the rest of 2009 and into 2010, CPI inflation will continue to be driven by external factors, especially higher oil and food commodity prices in world markets. In

comparison, domestic sources of inflationary pressures will be restrained by subdued factor costs, reflecting the temporary slack in the labour market and upcoming supply of commercial space. Nevertheless, these costs are expected to pick up in the latter half of next year as the recovery progresses. CPI inflation is likely to be around 0 per cent in 2009, before rising to 1–2 per cent in 2010. The MAS underlying inflation measure, which excludes accommodation and private road transport costs, is expected to come in around the same range.[2]

Monetary Policy

6.   Against continuing weakness and uncertainties in the external economic environment, the strength of the recovery in the Singapore economy is expected to be moderate beyond the initial uplift. While there could be some upward pressures on consumer prices emanating from higher global oil and food prices, underlying domestic cost pressures will be contained.

7.   MAS will therefore maintain the current policy stance of a zero per cent appreciation of the SG$NEER policy path. There will be no change to the width of the policy band and the level at which it is centred. MAS will continue to be vigilant over developments in the external environment including the medium-term risk of stronger global inflationary pressures.

****

Date: 14 April 2009

Introduction

1. In October 2008, MAS shifted its policy stance to a zero per cent appreciation of the SG$NEER policy band. The decision was taken amidst easing external and domestic inflationary pressures, and a weakening global economic environment.
2. Since the last policy review, the SG$NEER (Figure 2) has largely fluctuated in the lower half of the policy band. This reflected a number of factors, including the

FIGURE 2

Nominal Effective Exchange Rate (SG$NEER)

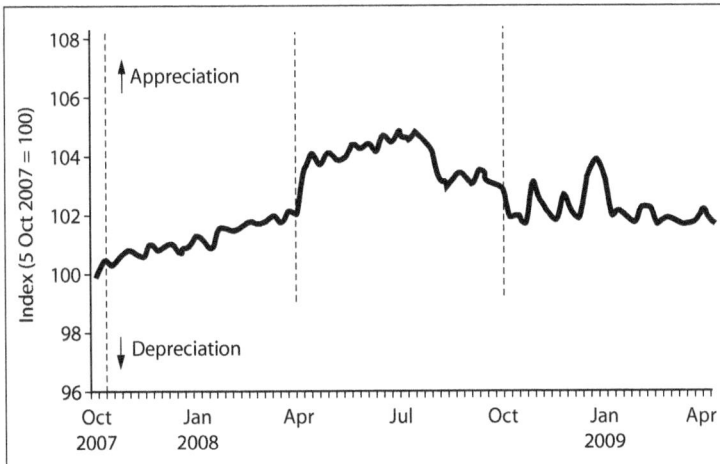

- - - - - indicates release of Monetary Policy Statement.

Reproduced with the permission of the Monetary Authority of Singapore © 2008 and 2009 The Monetary Authority of Singapore.

general strength of the US$, continued risk aversion by global investors and the erosion in domestic economic conditions. With the fall in global interest rates, the domestic three-month interbank rate also declined, from 1.88 per cent in September 2008 to 0.69 per cent at end-March 2009.

Outlook for 2009

3. The Singapore economy recorded a broad-based contraction of 16.4 per cent on a quarter-on-quarter seasonally adjusted annualised (q-o-q SAAR) basis in Q4-2008. Amidst the unprecedented collapse in global demand, trade-related activities such as manufacturing, wholesale trade and transport services decelerated sharply, while the financial sector was adversely affected by the turmoil in international financial markets. According to the Advance Estimates released by the Ministry of Trade and Industry today, GDP contracted by a further 19.7 per cent q-o-q SAAR in Q1-2009, with the decline accentuated by a reduction in pharmaceutical output. Both electronics manufacturing and financial services experienced a slower rate of contraction in early 2009 compared to Q4-2008.

4. Looking ahead, some moderation in the rate of decline in economic activity around the world is expected following the steep fall since the end of last year. A number of leading indicators have recently picked up slightly, and consumption spending has held up somewhat better than expected, particularly in the US.

While this is encouraging, considerable downside risks to growth remain. Job losses have been significant, and segments of the broader credit market continue to be impaired. Against this backdrop and in view of the sharp fall in domestic economic output over the past two quarters, Singapore's GDP growth forecast for 2009 has been lowered to between –9 per cent and –6 per cent.

5. In the meantime, CPI inflation has slowed significantly to 2.4 per cent year-on-year in Jan-Feb 2009, from 5.4 per cent in Q4 last year. This was largely due to the sharp decline in the prices of direct oil-related items, such as petrol, as well as a moderation in food price increases. In addition, price increases of several retail items such as clothing and household durables have eased. CPI inflation will continue to fall in the coming months, reflecting a combination of lower commodity prices and increased slack in the domestic economy. Domestic cost pressures are moderating, as evidenced by the fall in rentals and more subdued wage increases. With the high base in 2008, headline inflation would temporarily turn negative in certain months this year. For the whole of 2009, the CPI inflation forecast is unchanged at –1 per cent to 0 per cent.[3]

Monetary Policy

6. Amidst the global downturn and continuing stresses in world financial markets, external and domestic inflationary pressures are dissipating. Meanwhile, the

domestic economy is likely to remain below potential till a decisive recovery is seen in Singapore's export markets.

7.   In our assessment, the current level of the SG$NEER is appropriate for maintaining domestic price stability over the medium term, taking into account the prospects for growth in the Singapore economy. MAS will therefore re-centre the exchange rate policy band to the prevailing level of the SG$NEER, while keeping the zero per cent appreciation path. The width of the band will remain unchanged. The Singapore economy continues to be anchored by sound fundamentals and a resilient financial system. There is therefore no reason for any undue weakening of the Singapore dollar.

****

Date: 10 October 2008

Introduction

1.   MAS has maintained the policy of a modest and gradual appreciation of the Singapore dollar nominal effective exchange rate (SG$NEER) policy band since April 2004. In October 2007, the policy was tightened through a slight increase in the slope of the band, following which the policy band was re-centred at the

Reproduced with the permission of the Monetary Authority of Singapore © 2008 and 2009 The Monetary Authority of Singapore.

then-prevailing level of the SG$NEER in April 2008.
The policy stance has helped to mitigate inflationary
pressures amidst sustained economic growth and rising
global commodity prices.

2. The SG$NEER had fluctuated in the upper half
of the policy band between April and July 2008,
before easing since August against a broad-based
strengthening of the US$. (Figure 3) The pull-back
of the SG$NEER also reflected heightened domestic
growth concerns and a moderation of inflationary
pressures.

3. Meanwhile, domestic interbank rates edged lower in
tandem with the stronger SG$ following the April

FIGURE 3
Nominal Effective Exchange Rate (SG$NEER)

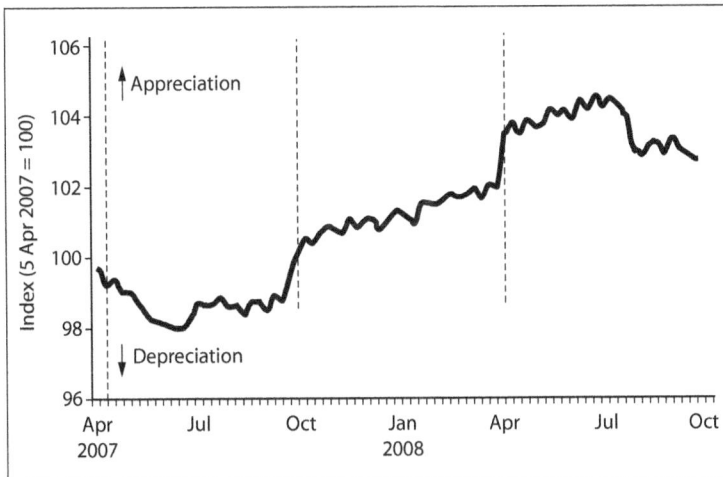

- - - - - indicates release of Monetary Policy Statement.

monetary policy announcement. More recently, the strain in global money markets caused the domestic three-month interbank rate to increase temporarily, but it has since eased to 1.88 per cent at end-September.

Outlook for 2008 and 2009

4. The Singapore economy has weakened over the course of 2008, alongside an escalation in the turmoil in financial markets and a more severe deceleration in global economic activity. The Advance Estimates released by the Ministry of Trade and Industry today show that Singapore's GDP declined by 6.3 per cent on a quarter-on-quarter seasonally adjusted annualised basis in Q3-2008. On a year-ago basis, activity also contracted mildly. The slowdown was generally broad based as external shocks were transmitted to the domestic economy via both the financial and trade channels. Nonetheless, certain industries, such as transport & storage, information and communications, and bank intermediation, continued to hold up, providing some support to GDP growth.

5. Looking ahead, the outlook for the global economy has deteriorated amidst heightened risk aversion and deleveraging in the financial sector. After a brief rebound in Q2-2008, economic conditions in the US have worsened as the effects of the fiscal stimulus package dissipated. The Japanese and Eurozone economies contracted in Q2-2008 and near-term conditions remain difficult. Economies in

Asia, including China and India, are also expected to slow.

6. These developments have presented new uncertainties for the Singapore economy. The risks to external demand conditions continue to be on the downside, and a more severe global downturn cannot be discounted. Slower growth in Asia will restrain activity in a range of services industries in Singapore such as transport-hub and tourism. Against this less favourable environment, Singapore's GDP growth forecast for 2008 has been revised from 4–5 per cent to around 3 per cent. Economic growth will likely remain below its potential rate over the next few quarters. Prospects of a recovery in the latter half of 2009 will depend significantly on how conditions evolve in the G3 and regional economies.

7. CPI inflation has peaked, declining from 7.5 per cent in Q2-2008 to 6.5 per cent in July-August on a year-on-year basis. In addition, it has fallen on a quarter-on-quarter basis, easing from 2.1 per cent in Q1 to 1.4 per cent in Q2 and 1.1 per cent in July-August. The sequential fall in CPI inflation reflects a moderation of both external and domestic price pressures. Externally, the recent sharp decline in commodity prices has helped to dampen global inflation. Domestically, the effects of past monetary policy tightening measures and the slowing economy have alleviated price pressures and eased resource constraints. Cost pressures have begun to recede, as evidenced by the recent fall in commercial rentals and more subdued wage increases.

8.   CPI inflation is projected to come within the 6–7 per cent forecast range in 2008, while the MAS underlying inflation measure, which excludes accommodation and private road transport costs, is expected to be 5–6 per cent. Over the coming months and into early 2009, the headline inflation rate will continue to be impacted by the pass-through of some earlier domestic cost increases. Nevertheless, CPI inflation is expected to trend down in 2009 as the global and domestic economies slow and for the year as a whole it is forecast to moderate to 2.5–3.5 per cent, with the MAS underlying inflation coming down to around 2 per cent.

Monetary Policy

9.   Against the backdrop of a weakening external economic environment and continuing stresses in global financial markets, the growth of the Singapore economy is expected to remain below potential in the period ahead. Concomitantly, external and domestic inflationary pressures are likely to ease.

10. MAS is therefore shifting its policy stance to a zero per cent appreciation of the SG$NEER policy band. This policy maintains the current level of the policy band, and there will be no re-centring of the band or change to its width. MAS stands ready to intervene to dampen excessive volatility in the SG$NEER should this become necessary. MAS will also continue to closely monitor developments in the external environment and their impact on the Singapore economy.

Notes

1. The 2009 GDP growth forecast was revised to –6 per cent to –4 per cent during the release of Advance Estimates for Q2 2009 GDP on 14 Jul 2009.
2. This forecast does not take into account any potential revision to the HDB Annual Value (AV), which would impact the headline CPI inflation forecast, but not that of the MAS underlying inflation rate.
3. The 2009 CPI inflation forecast was revised to –1.0 per cent to 0 per cent at MTI's Annual Economic Survey media briefing on 21 Jan 2009.

APPENDIX II
Key Budget FY2009 Initiatives

**Presented to Parliament by Finance Minister
Tharman Shanmugaratnam on 22 January 2009**

Keeping Jobs,
Building for the Future

Benefits for Businesses

Jobs for Singaporeans

(A) Jobs credit

To sustain jobs for Singaporeans, the Government will introduce a Jobs Credit, which will encourage businesses to preserve jobs in the downturn. This is a temporary scheme to help companies through an exceptional downturn. Details of the scheme are as follows:

- Employers will receive a 12 per cent cash grant on the first SG$2,500 of each month's wages for each employee on their CPF payroll.
- The Jobs Credit is for one year, and employers will receive the Jobs Credit in four payments: March, June, September and December 2009.
- For each payment, employers will receive Jobs Credits on the employees that are on their CPF

payrolls at the start of the quarter in which the payment is made. The wages paid to these employees in the previous quarter will be the qualifying wages used to calculate the 12 per cent cash credit that employers will receive.

○ For example, for the first payment to be received at the end of March 2009, businesses will receive Jobs Credit on the employees that are on their payrolls in January 2009. The wages paid to these employees in October to December 2008 will be the qualifying wages used to calculate the 12 per cent cash credit that employers will receive.

(B) Spur for workers and professionals

To help Singaporeans upgrade their skills so that they can stay employed or seek re-employment, the Government launched the Skills Programme for Upgrading and Resilience (SPUR), which provided higher course fee support for companies and individuals and absentee payrolls for companies that send their workers for training.

The Government will make the following enhancements to SPUR to help PMETs re-train:

• Course fee subsidies for PMET-level courses that are eligible for SPUR will be increased from 80 per cent to 90 per cent, the same subsidy level as rank-and-file level courses. This includes all Specialist and Advanced Diplomas offered by the polytechnics.

- Selected tertiary courses at UniSIM and the three publicly funded universities will be included under SPUR.

(C) Workfare Income Supplement (WIS) special payment

The Government will give low-income workers a temporary WIS Special Payment to supplement their pay and encourage them to stay employed. The WIS Special Payment will provide low-income workers with an additional 50 per cent of the WIS payments that they will receive over the course of this year.

The Government will also relax the work eligibility criteria of the WIS Special Payment, in order to enable more low-wage workers, particularly those with less regular employment, to benefit.

(D) Government hiring

The Government will be expanding recruitment. In total, 18,000 public sector jobs (including Government-supported jobs outside of the Government in areas such as childcare, tertiary education, and restructured hospitals) are expected to be available over the next two years. This includes about:

- 7,500 jobs in teaching positions and teaching support staff;
- 4,500 healthcare professionals and hospital administrative staff;

- 1,400 jobs for the Home Team;
- 2,000 jobs for MINDEF (including the SAF); and
- 2,600 for the rest of the Public Service.

Stimulating Bank Lending

(A) Special Risk-Sharing Initiative (SRI)

The Government will launch the Special Risk-Sharing Initiative (SRI) to ensure that viable companies continue to have access to credit to sustain their operations and keep jobs. The SRI will help extend Government support to a broader segment of the credit market, especially mid-sized companies, and share in the risks of trade financing for the first time.

The SRI has the following two components:

1. The New Bridging Loan Programme (BLP)
2. Trade Finance Schemes
   a. Loan Insurance Scheme — Plus (LIS+)
   b. Trade Credit Insurance Programme (TCIP)

The programmes under the SRI will be in operation for one year, but with possible extension for another year if the situation warrants.

(1) The New Bridging Loan Programme (BLP)

Commencing on 1 February 2009, the new Bridging Loan Programme (BLP) focuses on the needs of all companies, and especially the mid-sized companies, by improving their access to working capital.

Details of the BLP are as follows:

Structure	Details
Use of Funds	Working capital, including unsecured credit
Interest Rate	Minimum of 5 per cent The Participating Financing Institutions (PFIs) have the flexibility to charge interest rates above 5 per cent, and interest spreads above 5 per cent accure fully to the PFIs[1]
Maximum Loan Quantum	SG$5 million per borrower group
Eligible Companies	All locally-owned companies, and foreign-owned SMEs[2]
Risk Share	Government: 80 per cent Participating Financial Institution (PFI): 20 per cent

[1] Previously, 50 per cent of the interest rate spreads above 5 per cent accrued to the Government in exchange for taking on 50 per cent of the risk
[2] A foreign-owned SME is defined as a company with less than 30 per cent local shareholding, which also: (a) has maximum SG$15million Fixed Asset Investments (FAI); (b) is incorporated in Singapore; (c) is tax resident of Singapore; and (d) has at least one individual shareholder directly holding at least 10 per cent of total number of issued ordinary shares.

(2) Trade Finance Schemes

To address constraints of limited private insurance capacity and a reduced risk appetite, the Government will take on a significant proportion of the risks in trade financing.

Companies with orders need loans to fulfill their orders as well as insurance against the risk of their buyers defaulting on payments. The new trade finance schemes will help mid-sized and large exporters obtain loans and trade insurance on the scale they need.

Under SRI, there are two schemes, which address the trade finance component:

    a. Loan Insurance Scheme — Plus (LIS+)

    b. Trade Credit Insurance Programme (TCIP)

(a) *New Loan Insurance Scheme — Plus (LIS+)*

- LIS+ helps Singapore-based companies to secure working capital and trade financing facilities by providing private insurance to banks against default by borrowers.
- Commencing on 1 February 2009, details of the Scheme are as follows:

Structure	*Details*
Use of Funds	Secured working capital (e.g. against receivables)
Maximum Loan Quantum	SG$15 million per borrower group
Eligible Companies	All companies (at least 30 per cent local shareholding)
Risk Share (for qualifying loans)	Government: 75 per cent PFI: 25 per cent

(b) *New Trade Credit Insurance Programme (TCIP)*

- To protect Singapore-based companies against non-payment by buyers, a new Trade Credit Insurance

Programme (TCIP) will be launched in March 2009.
- The Government is examining ways to increase the insurance coverage capacity. Also, to ameliorate the rising insurance premium costs, the government will be subsidising part of the insurance premiums.
- More details will be announced in MTI's COS

(B) Enhancements to existing credit measures

The Government will enhance existing loan schemes. These enhancements will [be] in effect for one year, starting 1 February 2009.

(B1) Local Enterprise Finance Scheme (LEFS)

For loans made under LEFS, the Government will increase its risk-share for loans made to local non-SMEs, from 50 per cent to 80 per cent. This will be similar to the Government risk-share for LEFS loans made to SMEs.

(B2) Micro Loan Programme (MLP)

For loans made under the MLP, the Government will increase its risk-share, from 80 per cent to 90 per cent.

(B3) Internationalisation Finance Scheme

The Government will increase the maximum loan quantum per borrower group, from SG$15 million to SG$50 million.

(C) Other credit-related measures

(C1) Extension of Tax Deduction on Loan Loss Provisions for Banks

To encourage banks to continue making adequate loan impairment provisions and bolster their financial strength to underpin continued lending in the downturn, the Government will extend the tax deduction on loss provisions made pursuant to MAS Notice 612, as well as other equivalent MAS notices for finance companies and merchant banks, for a further three Years of Assessment.

Enhancing Business Cashflow and Competitiveness

(A) Easing business cash-flow

(A1) Property Tax Rebate for Industrial and Commercial Properties

The Government will provide a 40 per cent property tax rebate for industrial and commercial properties for 2009. The Government strongly urges landlords to pass on the benefits of this rebate to their tenants.

(A2) Rental Rebates by JTC, HDB, and SLA

JTC, HDB, and SLA will provide a 15 per cent rental rebate to their tenants and land lessees, exceeding the savings due to the property tax rebate. JTC, HDB, and SLA will be releasing the details of these concessions separately on 22 January 2009. The rental rebate will also be extended to stallholders who are paying market rents in markets and food centres managed by NEA.

(A3) Enhancements to Loss Carry-Back Scheme

To help businesses with their cash-flow, the loss *carry-back* relief system will be enhanced for Years of Assessment 2009 and 2010. The cap on losses that can be claimed against past taxable income is increased to SG$200,000 from SG$100,000. Businesses will also be allowed to claim losses against the taxable income of their preceding three Years of Assessment, instead of just the immediate preceding year as under the current scheme. IRAS will allow claims for the tax refund to be based on a declaration of estimated losses. This will allow businesses to obtain their cash refunds on taxes paid in previous years instead of having to wait for the finalisation of their chargeable income and taxes.

(A4) Tax exemption on Remittance of Foreign-Sourced Income

To enable businesses to make best use of all their sources of funds to meet their financing needs in Singapore during this time of credit tightness, the Government will temporarily expand the scope of the Foreign-Sourced Income Exemption scheme to cover all foreign-sourced income, and not just foreign-sourced dividends, branch profits and service income. The Government will also temporarily lift the conditions that are currently required for foreign-sourced income to be exempted from tax when remitted to Singapore. With these temporary enhancements, businesses will be exempt from tax on the foreign-sourced income that they remit between 22 Jan 2009 to 21 January 2010 (both dates inclusive), provided that the remitted income is earned on or before 21 January 2009.

(A5) Transport Rebates and Concessions

The Government will grant the following rebates and concessions on transport-related taxes and fees:

- A 30 per cent road tax rebate for goods vehicles, buses and taxis for one year. This rebate will take effect on 1 July 2009.
- A 20 per cent concession in port dues to be granted to all harbour craft (except pleasure craft for personal use) which will help local companies engaged in commercial activities within Singapore's port waters. This concession will be for one year and will take effect on 1 April 2009.
- An increase in aircraft landing fee rebate from 15 per cent to 25 per cent for 2009.
- Extension of the special tax exemption for Compressed Natural Gas (CNG) vehicles until December 2011. From 2012 onwards, the CNG special tax will be removed and replaced with a CNG duty of SG$0.20 per kilogramme of CNG.

(A6) Further Extension of the Government Fee Freeze

The Government will extend the freeze on Government Fees and Charges to December 2009. This will include fees charged on all Government provided services, charges in public carparks, and all license fees. (Regulatory charges, such as those in the transport sector and the development charges applied in the property market, will not be frozen. The Government fee freeze is not applied to fees charged by non-government entities, such as the universities, restructured hospitals and town councils.)

(A7) Measures for Property Developers

Many developers are planning to hold back developments that they had originally planned. To support developers in doing so, the Government will introduce the following measures:

- Defer property tax for commercial developers for land approved for development for up to two years. Land approved for development refers to land with a valid Provisional or Written Permission granted by the URA. The property tax deferral will take effect from 22 January 2009 or the date of Provisional or Written Permission, whichever is later. The deferral will lapse on 21 January 2011, or at Temporary Occupation Permit (TOP), or date of transfer of the land, whichever is the earliest.
- Allow a one-year extension of the project completion period for private residential projects. This would give flexibility to developers to phase out their projects in the current uncertain market conditions.
- Allow re-assignment of Government sale sites and private land owned by foreign housing developers for applications made by 22 January 2010.

- Extend the period for developers to dispose of all residential units from two years to four years. Developers may also rent out unsold residential units for a maximum of four years to mitigate holding costs.

(A8) Deferment of Increase in Assessment Rate for Hotels

The Government will defer the increase in assessment rate for hotel rooms, which was due to increase to 25 per cent on 1 January 2009, by one year. Hence, the assessment rate for hotel rooms will remain at 20 per cent for 2009.

(B) Reducing taxes to encourage investments

(B1) Corporate Income Tax (CIT) Rate Cut

To promote Singapore's competitiveness, the Government will reduce the CIT rate from 18 per cent to 17 per cent. This reduction will take effect from the Year of Assessment 2010.

(B2) Accelerated Capital Allowance (CA)

Currently, businesses can generally write down the costs incurred for the acquisition of plants and machinery on a three-year straight line basis. To support businesses intending to invest in preparation for the recovery, the Government will allow plant and machinery acquired during the financial years ended 2009 and 2010 to qualify for an accelerated write-down. This temporarily accelerated write-down will allow businesses to write down the costs of these newly acquired plants and machinery within two years with 75 per cent of the write-down taking place in the first year of CA claim alone.

(B3) Writing Down of Renovation and Refurbishment Expenses

To encourage especially small businesses in the service sector to refit their business premises this year and the next, the Government will allow businesses to temporarily write-down qualifying expenses incurred on renovation and refurbishment of business premises fully within one year, instead of the current three years. This concession will apply to qualifying renovation and refurbishment expenses incurred during the financial years ended 2009 and 2010. The current cap on the amount of qualifying renovation and refurbishment expenses that can be written down will remain at SG$150,000 every three years per business entity.

(B4) New Tax Framework for Corporate Amalgamations

In a corporate amalgamation, the amalgamated company takes over all assets and liabilities of the amalgamating companies, and the amalgamating companies cease to exist. Under the existing tax treatment, when assets and liabilities are transferred upon amalgamation, tax consequences are often triggered as the amalgamating companies are treated as having ceased business and disposed of their assets and liabilities, and the amalgamated company having acquired or commenced a new business. So, for instance, plant and machinery are treated to have been sold by the amalgamating companies to the amalgamated company.

To make it easier for companies to restructure and rationalise, the Government will introduce a tax framework for qualifying corporate amalgamations. This framework will alleviate the tax cost associated with corporate amalgamations. A public consultation will be held in February 2009 to seek views on this new tax framework for qualifying corporate amalgamations.

(C) Sector specific taxes and duties

For financial sector activities

(C1) Enhancements to and Streamlining of Fund Management Incentives

Currently, under the fund management incentives, there are conditions such as the fund cannot be 100 per cent beneficially owned by resident investors and there are limits placed on the holdings by resident corporate investors in these funds. The Government will now remove all these limits on qualifying funds so that they can accept investments freely from resident corporates, in addition to resident individuals. This will allow our resident corporates to enjoy the full benefits of tax exemption on qualifying income derived by the funds, thus encouraging resident corporates to have more of their monies managed by funds in Singapore.

This enhancement of the fund management incentives will also apply to qualifying funds that are constituted in the form of Limited Partnerships. A qualifying fund is one which, amongst other conditions, has at least SG$50 million under management at the point of application for the tax incentive. Fund managers may apply for the scheme with effect from 1 April 2009. Both the existing and enhanced fund management incentives will also be subject to review after five years. MAS will release the details by April 2009.

(C2) Recovery of GST for Qualifying Local Funds

To promote fund administration and fund management in Singapore, the Government will allow qualifying funds that are managed by a prescribed fund manager in Singapore to recover a substantial portion of the GST incurred on prescribed expenses. This change will be in place from 22 January 2009 to 31 March 2014 (both dates inclusive). MAS will release the details by April 2009.

(C3) Expansion of Scope of Tax Exemption under Fund Management and Trust Incentives

The Government will enhance the lists of specified income and designated investments under the fund management and trusts incentives, thus expanding the scope of tax exemption. For instance, amount payable on qualifying Islamic debt securities will be included in the list of specified income. The enhancements will take effect from 22 January 2009. MAS will release the details by April 2009.

(C4) Enhancements to Financial Sector Incentive — Headquarter Services (FSI-HQ) Scheme

To promote Singapore as the choice location for headquarter functions of financial institutions, the Government will enhance the FSI-HQ scheme by granting withholding tax exemption on interest payable on qualifying loans taken by an FSI-HQ company. The Government will also subsume the current tax incentive scheme for provision of these processing services under the FSI-HQ scheme, thus allowing FSI-HQs to enjoy incentivised income from their provision of high value-added processing services. These enhancements will be effective from 22 January 2009 to 31 December 2013 (both dates inclusive). MAS will release the details by April 2009.

(C5) Extension and Enhancement of Commodity Derivatives Traders (CDT) scheme

To encourage the growth of derivative trading activities in Singapore, the Government will extend the CDT scheme (which is due to expire on 26 February 2009) and subsume it under a new Derivatives Market (Commodity Derivatives Trader) award under the Financial Sector Incentive scheme. The Government will also lift existing counterparty restrictions for trades carried out on exchanges under this scheme. These changes will be effective from 27 February 2009 to 31 December 2013 (both dates inclusive). MAS will release the details by April 2009.

For Maintenance, Repair and Overhaul (MRO) activities

(C6) Zero-Rating for the Aerospace Industry

To support the growth of the Maintenance, Repair and Overhaul (MRO) industry in Singapore, the Government will expand the scope of qualifying aircraft to include all aircraft, including private aircraft, which is wholly used or intended to be wholly used for international transportation of goods and passengers. This is in line with the zero-rating of international transportation.

To ease GST compliance costs for the MRO industry, zero-rating is also extended to cover the sale, maintenance or repair services of aircraft components or systems, as long as they form part of a qualifying aircraft. A new scheme will be introduced to facilitate the import of aircraft components or systems for qualifying aircraft without GST.

These changes will take effect from 1 April 2009. IRAS will release the details by March 2009.

For auction, exhibition and specialised storage activities

(C7) Suspension of GST and Duty on Goods Temporarily Removed from Zero-GST or Licensed Warehouses

To encourage the growth of the auction and exhibition industry, as well as specialised storage facilities, the Government will, with effect from 1 April 2009, suspend

GST and duty on goods (including wine) that are temporarily removed from a zero-GST or Licensed warehouse for auctions or exhibitions, even if the goods are sold during the auction or exhibition, provided that the goods are returned to the warehouses subsequently. Singapore Customs will release the details by March 2009.

For wine trading activities

(C8) Exemption of Duty to Facilitate Wine Trading Activities

To promote wine trading activities and help develop the wine industry in Singapore, the Government will exempt duty and provide GST relief for a specified quantity of wine for use at approved wine exhibitions and conference events with effect from 1 April 2009. Singapore Customs will release the details by March 2009.

For maritime activities

(C9) Withholding Tax Exemption for Maritime Industry

To give support to the maritime industry, the Government will extend the withholding tax exemption on interest payable on qualifying loans taken by shipping enterprises to acquire vessels which are registered with the Singapore Registry of Ships under the Block Transfer Scheme, subject to conditions. This extension will be for a further period of five years with effect from 1 January 2009.

(D) Making innovation pervasive

(D1) Accelerated Writing-Down Allowance (WDA) for acquisition of Intellectual Property (IP) rights for Media and Digital Entertainment (MDE) content

To encourage media and digital entertainment (MDE) businesses to create and exploit their intellectual property from Singapore, the Government will enhance the current WDA incentive to allow MDE businesses to write down the costs of their qualifying IP rights for MDE content in two years, instead of five years. This accelerated write-down will apply for qualifying IP for MDE content acquired between 22 January 2009 and 31 October 2013 (both dates inclusive).

(D2) Test-Bedding Fund

To further encourage creation and test-bedding of new ideas, the Government will put SG$200 million in a Test-Bedding Fund to make Singapore a "living lab" for companies and entrepreneurs to nurture new ideas, test innovative solutions and develop future global businesses. The fund will be managed by the Economic Development Board (EDB).

(D3) Government Taking the Lead in Innovation

In 2008, the Government set up the Core Innovation Fund to help private companies collaborate directly with government agencies to develop innovative solutions for public services. We will set aside SG$180 million in the fund over the next two years. In addition, the Government will be more proactive in seeking collaboration with the private sector, through the use of Calls-for-Collaboration (CFC). This will bring clusters of companies together to develop solutions for government agencies, businesses and the public.

Benefits for Households

Supporting Families

The Resilience Package will provide additional support for families and the community during this downturn. The key benefit that Singaporeans will derive from the package will come from the effort to preserve jobs through the Jobs initiatives — the Jobs Credit, the Workfare Income Supplement Scheme (WIS) Special Payment and Skills Programme for Upgrading and Resilience (SPUR). The Government will also complement the Jobs initiatives with the following:

- Direct assistance to households
- Targeted help for the most vulnerable groups
- Support for charitable giving and the community

(A) Direct assistance to households

(A1) Goods and Services Tax (GST) Credits and Senior Citizens' Bonus

To help households cope with their cash-flow problems arising from unemployment or reduced incomes, the Government will double the GST Credits and Senior Citizen's Bonus that citizens will receive in 2009.

This additional tranche will be paid on 1 March 2009 and will be on top of what citizens will receive in July 2009 as part of the 2007 GST Offset Package. About 2.4 million Singaporeans are eligible for the GST Credits including about 734,000 elderly Singaporeans who will also benefit from the Senior Citizen's Bonus.

The amount of GST Credits and Senior Citizens' Bonus citizens can receive in 2009 will like the previous year depend on:

(i)   The Annual Value (AV) of their residence in 2008;[1]
(ii) Their Assessable Income (AI) for Year of Assessment 2008; and
(iii) Their age in the year of payout.

Payout Structure

AI \ AV	< 6,000	$6,001 to $11,000	> $11,000
Up to $24,000	$250 × 2 Aged 55–59: $400 × 2 Aged 60 and above: $500 × 2	$200 × 2 Aged 55–59: $300 × 2 Aged 60 and above: $400 × 2	$100 × 2 Aged 55–59: $150 × 2 Aged 60 and above: $200 × 2
$24,001–$100,000			
More than $100,000		$100*	
NSFs/NS men		$100#	

* If an individual has already received a payout in previous years, he will not receive the $100.

NSFs/NSmen will receive the $100 only in the year that they first qualify.

(A2) Service and Conservancy Charges (S&CC) Rebates

The Government will provide an additional one month of S&CC Rebates to those living in a one-room to three-room HDB flats, who will therefore receive a total of three to 4.5 months for this year. Those in four-room HDB to Executive apartments will receive an additional half-month, or a total of one to two months of rebates. The additional S&CC rebate will be paid in April 2009.

Altogether, about 800,000 eligible HDB households will benefit from the rebates.

Payout Quantum (Number of Months)

	1-R	2-R	3-R	4-R	5-R	HDB Executive
Mar 2009	1	0.5	0.5	0.5	—	—
Apr 2009	**+1**	**+1**	**+1**	**+0.5**	**+0.5**	**+0.5**
Jun 2009	1	0.5	0.5	0.5	0.5	0.5
Sep 2009	1	0.5	0.5	—	—	—
Dec 2009	0.5	0.5	0.5	0.5	0.5	—
Calendar Year Total	**4.5**	**3**	**3**	**2**	**1.5**	**1.0**

(A3) Rental Rebates

The Government will provide an additional month of rental rebates in 2009, to eligible households in public rental flats. The additional rebate, to be paid in March and December 2009, will supplement the existing rental rebates these low-income families are already receiving as part of the 2007 GST Offset Package.

In total, about 35,000 eligible households in public rental flats are expected to benefit from the rebates.

Payout Quantum (Number of Months)

	1-R	*2-R*
Mar 2009	0.5+**0.5**	0.5+**0.5**
Jun 2009	1	0.5
Sep 2009	1	0.5
Dec 2009	0.5+**0.5**	0.5+**0.5**
Calendar Year Total	4	3

(A4) Personal Income Tax Rebate

The Government will give a personal income tax rebate of 20 per cent (capped at SG$2,000) for tax-residents for Year of Assessment 2009. This will provide an immediate reduction in the tax payable for these individuals for last year's income.

(A5) Installment Option for Personal Income Tax Payment

To help tide taxpayers over the current difficult economic situation, the Government is allowing individual tax-residents who have lost their jobs in 2008 or lose their jobs in 2009 to pay their personal income taxes for year of assessment 2009 in monthly instalments of up to 24 months, up from the current 12 months allowed. Affected taxpayers can apply to IRAS for this extended instalment assistance.

(A6) Property Tax Rebate

The Government is providing a 40 per cent property tax rebate for owner-occupied residential properties for 2009.

(A7) Removal of Tax on Net Annual Value of Property

Currently, taxpayers are required to pay income tax on the Net Annual Value of their dwelling or secondary residences. However, an exemption of up to SG$150,000 of Net Annual Value for one owner-occupied residential property is granted.

The Government will remove this income tax on Net Annual Value of residential property with effect from Year of Assessment 2010.

(A8) Increase in Additional CPF Housing Grant

The Government will enhance the Additional CPF Housing Grant (AHG) for first time home-buyers. The maximum AHG quantum will be increased from SG$30,000 to SG$40,000. At the same time, the household income ceiling will be increased from SG$4,000 to SG$5,000.

(A9) Other measures

On top of the 2009 measures, households will also benefit from the following measures, which were announced as part of the 2007 GST Offset Package.

Utilities-Save (U-Save) Rebates: Eligible households will receive U-Save rebates of SG$70 to SG$210 in 2009. This will benefit around 800,000 HDB households.

Payout Quantum

	1-R	2-R	3-R	4-R	5-R	HDB Executive
Jan 2009	SG$110	SG$110	SG$100	SG$95	SG$60	SG$40
Jul 2009	SG$100	SG$100	SG$90	SG$85	SG$50	SG$30
Calendar Year Total	SG$210	SG$210	SG$190	SG$180	SG$110	SG$70

Post-Secondary Education Account (PSEA) top-up: Young Singaporeans aged 7 to 20 will receive a top-up of $100 to $400 to their Post-Secondary Education Accounts (PSEA) in 2009. Those who are older and from less well-off families will get a higher top-up to their PSEA.

AV Age	Up to SG$10,000	> SG$10,000
7 to 12	SG$200	SG$100
13 to 20	SG$400	SG$200

(B) Targeted Help for the Most Vulnerable Groups

(B1) Public Transport Fund (PTF) Top-up

The Government will top-up the Public Transport Fund to SG$10 million to provide public transport vouchers for all low-income households who need help.

(B2) Financial Assistance Schemes for Education

To provide every encouragement to students whose families face financial difficulties during the economic downturn, the Ministry of Education (MOE) will enhance the financial assistance schemes for students in our schools, and introduce a Short-Term Study Assistance Scheme (SSAS) for students in our ITEs, polytechnics and autonomous universities.

(B3) Public Assistance Rate

The Government will increase the Public Assistance Rate for single-person households by SG$30 per month to SG$360

(B4) Singapore Allowance

For government pensioners, the Government has decided to increase the Singapore Allowance by SG$20 per month to SG$240.

(C) Support for charitable giving and the community

(C1) Citizens' Consultative Committees (CCCs) ComCare Fund and Self-Help Groups (SHGs)

To enhance support for low-income households, the Government is increasing funding to the CCC ComCare Fund to SG$7 million a year, for the next two years. It will also increase funding to SHGs to SG$9 million a year, for the next two years.

(C2) Increased Tax Deduction and Additional Grant for Government Funded Voluntary Welfare Organisations (VWOs)

To encourage greater charitable giving this year, the Government will increase the tax deduction for donations made in 2009 to Institutions of Public Character (IPCs) and other approved institutions from 200 per cent to 250 per cent.

To support government-funded voluntary welfare organisations (VWOs), the Government will provide an additional SG$15 million in funding to them for one year (2009).

(C3) Extending business measures to VWOs

As VWOs also employ workers, the Government is extending the Jobs Credit provided to companies to all VWOs.

(C4) Extending Start-up Exemption to Companies Limited by Guarantee (CLGs)

To support the growth of Companies Limited by Guarantee set up by social entrepreneurs, the Government is extending the start-up tax exemption to Companies Limited by Guarantee. Under this exemption, qualifying start-ups can enjoy full tax exemption on their first $100,000 of chargeable income and 50 per cent exemption for the next SG$200,000, for their first three Years of Assessment. This extension will take effect from Year of Assessment 2010.

Other Initiatives

Building a Home for the Future

The Resilience Package provides a further boost to investments in making Singapore an extremely liveable global city and the best home for Singaporeans.

We are pushing ahead in four areas:

- Expanding and accelerating public sector infrastructural spending;
- Developing suburban nodes and rejuvenating our neighbourhoods;
- Pushing ahead on sustainable development;
- Spending more on our education and health infrastructure.

(A) Expanding and accelerating public sector infrastructure spending

The Government will increase public sector construction spending to between SG$18 billion and SG$20 billion in 2009. This is significantly higher than the SG$15 billion contracted in 2008 and SG$6 billion in 2007.

The increased spending arises from the planned ramp-up in infrastructure development, and bringing forward of SG$1.3 billion of projects to 2009. The Government had previously deferred some of these projects to avoid exacerbating the over-heating construction sector and adding pressure to construction costs for the economy. Others are projects which had been due over the next two to three years that the Government has decided to bring forward and comprise smaller infrastructure contracts worth up to SG$50 million each, which can be taken up by our small and medium-sized contractors.

(B) Developing suburban nodes and rejuvenating neighbourhoods

To develop both a distinctive business hub in the centre of the city and new suburban hubs that will decentralise economic activity and create jobs nearer to home, the Government will be:

- Investing in new regional commercial nodes such as Jurong Lake District, the new Kallang Riverside and Paya Lebar Central;
- Rejuvenating our public housing neighbourhoods, including enlivening the public spaces within our estates and pushing ahead with ABC Waters Programme;
- Linking together all parts of the island through a comprehensive road network and developing viable mass transit alternatives by expanding our rail networks;
- Spending more on basic amenities such as our drainage and sewerage network.

(C) Pushing ahead on sustainable development

The Government has over the last year been developing our sustainable development blueprint for Singapore. MEWR and MND will be discussing our thinking and plans in further detail during the Committee of Supply (COS).

In total, the Government plans to spend SG$1 billion over the next five years on sustainable development initiatives. The funds will support programmes such as energy efficiency for industry and households, green transport, clean energy and the greening of our living spaces.

(D) Spending more on education and healthcare

(D1) Enhancing School Education

To enhance education for our students, the Government will be upgrading the hardware and software of the education system, including:

- Providing better facilities for an all-round education in every school, and accelerating some projects like the roll-out of indoor sports halls;
- Enhancing both the size and quality of the teaching force; and
- Bringing in allied educators into our schools to collaborate with teachers in providing better attention for every child.

(D2) Expanding healthcare capacity

The Government is committing to a substantial expansion of the healthcare sector, including:
- Investing SG$4 billion over the next five years in healthcare infrastructure which will include the redevelopment of older hospitals, medical centres and a new hospital in the west, as well as seeing through

existing projects like the Khoo Teck Puat Hospital in the north;

- Building new community hospitals and boosting capabilities in treating chronic diseases (e.g. stroke, heart and kidney failure) and other age-related conditions (e.g. dementia);
- Enhancing capabilities for long-term care (including rehabilitation, home care and palliative services after patients have been discharged from hospitals); and
- Developing an electronic health records system that will be accessible by authorised medical practitioners at hospitals and polyclinics, and eventually extending to the community care sector.

Notes

1. This applies to Singaporeans whose NRIC address has changed in 2008, and newly eligible Singaporeans. For Singaporeans whose NRIC address has not changed, the amount of benefits will depend on the Annual Value (AV) of their residence in 2007.

APPENDIX III
Summary of the Economic Strategies Committee (ESC) Key Recommendations
1 February 2010

High-skilled People, Innovative Economy, Distinctive Global City

We must make skills, innovation and productivity the basis for sustaining Singapore's economic growth. This will also provide for inclusive growth, with a broad-based increase in the incomes of our citizens.

We must also be a vibrant and distinctive global city — open and diverse, the best place to grow and reach out to a rising Asia, and a home that provides an outstanding quality of life for our people.

ESC Key Recommendations

We must achieve higher productivity growth of 2 to 3 per cent per year, enabling our GDP to grow on average by 3 to 5 per cent per year over the next decade.

Increased productivity is not achieved merely through increased efficiency, but restructuring our economy to provide more room for rapidly growing and innovative enterprises.

7 Key Strategies

1. Growing through skills and innovation

    a. High-level national council to oversee and drive efforts to boost productivity and expand CET (Continuing Education and Training) to ensure national level coordination of government agencies and close collaboration between public and private sectors.

    b. Encourage enterprise innovation and investments in technology and training, both through broad-based and targeted sectoral approaches.

- Introduce strong economy-wide fiscal incentives for companies to invest in productivity enhancement and innovation.
- Set up a National Productivity Fund to provide grants to support industry-focused and enterprise-level productivity initiatives at the sectoral level.

    c. Upskill workers at all levels through enhanced CET system.

- Multiple skills-based progression pathways to complement academic route.
- Reach out to more PMETs.

d. Strengthen support for low-wage workers through enhanced Workfare Income Supplement (WIS) scheme, and additional support for training.

e. Manage our dependence on the foreign workforce by raising foreign worker levies in a gradual and phased manner.

- Also raise the quality of the foreign workforce and encourage employers to retain skilled foreign workers by increasing the skilled levy differential

2. Anchor Singapore as a Global-Asia Hub

a. A key Global-Asia hub for global players seeking to tap on opportunities offered by a rising Asia, and for Asian enterprises looking to expand beyond their home markets.

b. A globally competitive manufacturing sector at 20–25 per cent of the economy, with emphasis on knowledge-intensive manufacturing (e.g. bio-electronics), and taking advantage of the convergence of manufacturing and services (e.g. headquarter operations, clinical trials for new drugs and IP management services).

c. A trusted financial and modern services hub — through deepening existing capabilities in sectors such as ICT, financial, logistics services, and new areas such as consumer-centric intelligence.

d. A leading consumer business centre — where businesses gather consumer insights and test-bed products and services meant for a range of markets across Asia.

e. Location of choice to test-bed "future ready" urban solutions that can be exported to Asia and the world.

3. Build a Vibrant and Diverse Corporate Ecosystem

a. Develop a deeper base of globally competitive Singapore enterprises (to grow 1,000 Singapore enterprises with revenues over SG$100 million by 2020).

- Catalysing cross-border financing capacity: Plug gaps in financing capabilities through market-based solutions and institutions — aimed at providing risk and credit insurance for trade finance; guarantees for loans by commercial banks and guarantees and possible co-financing for project finance. This could involve establishing an EXIM bank-like specialist financial institution.

- Growth capital for growth-oriented enterprises: Seeding public-private investment fund to supply up to SG$1.5bn of new capital for growth-oriented SMEs based in Singapore in the next 10 years.

- Empowering Trade Associations and Chambers: Strengthen institutional capabilities to serve as industry champions and market facilitators for our companies to expand overseas.

b. Establish Singapore as [the] premier location in Asia for MNCs, global mid-sized companies, and Asian enterprises seeking to internationalise, through developing deeper market knowledge and expertise with a pan-Asian focus and facilitating their quick start-up and expansion.
   - Develop professional services and grow a pool of Asia-ready managers, professionals and leaders.
   - Shared resource centre and ready access to knowledge and networks.
c. Support strengthened alliances between MNCs and local SMEs to co-innovate, build track records, and internationalise.

4. Make Innovation Pervasive, and Strengthen Commercialisation of R&D

a. Grow R&D expenditure over the long-term. For [the] first half decade, increase Singapore's total expenditure on R&D to 3.5 per cent of GDP by 2015 (compared to 3 per cent currently) by growing private sector R&D.
   - Sustain public sector R&D commitment to create a strong value proposition for the private sector.
b. Strengthen emphasis on commercialisation of R&D through new innovation platforms (e.g. consortia-type cooperation between businesses in the same sector) and developing talent in downstream commercialisation e.g. patent agents.

c. Emphasise design-driven innovation through incentives for capabilities such as in product and industrial design, and provisions for affordable spaces for industry collaboration.

5. Become a Smart Energy Economy

a. Improve energy security and resilience with [sic.] through the diversification of energy sources
    • Study the feasibility of nuclear energy for the long-term.
    • Explore new sources such as coal and electricity import.
    • Continue to support the development of renewable energy sources.
b. Invest in critical economy-wide energy infrastructure
    • Intelligent Energy Systems (IES) to allow consumers to make informed choices about their energy consumption and develop.
    • Jurong Island as an energy-optimised industrial cluster.
c. Step up measures to promote energy efficiency in industry, buildings and transport.
d. Price energy to reflect real costs and constraints — to study how best to implement a carbon pricing scheme in anticipation of future carbon constraints should there be a global agreement on climate change.

6. Enhance Land Productivity to Secure Future Growth

a. Plan ahead for a new, vibrant waterfront city, size comparable to Marina Bay by rejuvenating existing port land at Tanjong Pagar, after the expiry of the port lease in 2027.

b. To study, under the Concept Plan 2011, the feasibility of a consolidated port at Tuas in the long term. If feasible, it will increase port efficiency by allowing the port to achieve greater economies of scale in terms of land and operations, and free up existing port land to support new economic activities in the future.

c. Increase land productivity and inject greater land use flexibility — intensify land use to support new and higher value activities; progressively rejuvenate of [sic.] mature industrial estates; and adopt greater flexibility in land zoning.

d. Enhance diversity of business locations to support a range of enterprise needs — introduce new locations for headquarter functions and new industries in Jurong Lake District and Kallang Riverside Precinct respectively

e. Invest ahead to create new underground spaces — develop an underground master plan, and create basement spaces in conjunction with new underground infrastructural projects, especially around our transport nodes.

7. **Build a Distinctive Global City and an Endearing Home**

    a. Attract and nurture a diverse pool of talent and develop thought and practice leadership
        - Provide talent here with opportunities to develop new peaks of excellence in diverse fields (e.g. arts, design, fashion, sports science) by developing or attracting new world class institutions and programmes.
        - Groom corporate and professional leaders by bringing in top-quality post graduate institutions and major corporate universities.
        - Adopt a talent-centric approach to attracting top quality people by providing agencies with more flexibility.
    b. Make Singapore a leading cultural capital
        - Create affordable spaces and incentives for the development of creative arts and design clusters.
        - Rejuvenate the Singapore Civic District as a premier arts and culture destination by strengthening programming, marketing, and linkages between cultural institutions in the district.
        - Develop artistic, professional, scholastic and technical capabilities in the arts, including development of reputable degree and research programmes.

c. Provide the best quality of life in Asia
   - Host more pinnacle international events.
   - Develop economically and socially vibrant districts through active place management.
   - Create highly-liveable precincts through new urban planning solutions and establish eco-precincts to model cutting-edge sustainable development strategies.

APPENDIX IV
Key Budget FY2010 Initiatives

**Presented to Parliament by Finance Minister
Tharman Shanmugaratnam on 22 February, 2010**

Benefits for Businesses

Raising Productivity: Skills, Innovation and Economic Restructuring

The Government will commit SG$1.1 billion a year over the next five years in the form of tax benefits, grants and training subsidies to support the national effort to raise productivity.

Details of the relevant Budget measures are given below.

(A) Boosting Skills and Enterprise Productivity through National Effort

(A1) National Productivity and Continuing Education Council (New)

The Government will establish a high-level National Productivity and Continuing Education Council. The Council will be chaired by DPM Teo Chee Hean and include members from the Government, business community and the labour movement. It will:

- Galvanise the major national effort to boost skills and enterprise productivity;
- Develop a comprehensive system for continuing education and training (CET); and
- Oversee the work of the different government agencies and promote close collaboration among the business sector, workers and unions, and the public sector.

More details on the composition of the Council and how it will approach its work will be announced later by DPM Teo.

(B) Investing in People

(B1) Expansion of the Continuing Education and Training (CET) System (Enhanced)

The Government will spend SG$2.5 billion over the next five years on CET.

The Government will build up an outstanding CET system for adults, to complement a first-rate education system for our young. This is our response to the next phase of gains in productivity, which will require us to develop competence in more complex tasks, mastery of skills and depth of expertise in every trade and profession.

(B2) Introduction of Workfare Training Scheme (WTS) (New)

The Government will introduce a three-year Workfare Training Scheme (WTS) to complement the Workfare Income Supplement (WIS) scheme. The WTS will:

- Subsidise 90 per cent to 95 per cent of absentee payroll and course fee outlay for employers, when they send their low-wage workers for training;
- Provide cash grants, capped at SG$400 per year, when WIS recipients complete their training;
- Introduce a structured training programme for those with very low skills, including those who are unemployed.

(B3) Enhancement of Workfare Income Supplement (Enhanced)

The Government will enhance the Workfare Income Supplement (WIS) Scheme as follows:

- *Higher payouts.* Maximum payouts for the WIS will be increased by between SG$150 and SG$400, with more going to older workers to encourage them to remain in the workforce; and
- *Extension to more workers.* The Government will extend WIS to workers earning up to SG$1,700 per month — up from the current limit of SG$1,500 per month.

Further details of the enhancements to Workfare (WIS and WTS) will be announced during the Ministry of Manpower's Committee of Supply.

(C) Supporting Enterprise Investments in Innovation and Productivity

The Government will provide tax incentives for businesses to invest in upgrading their operations and creating new value. The Government will also extend substantial grants to specific industries, clusters and enterprises.

(C1) Productivity and Innovation Credit (New)

Currently, only research and development (R&D) qualifies for additional tax deductions, of up to 150 per cent of expenditures. The Government will introduce the Productivity and Innovation Credit as a major enhancement, to spur a much broader range of innovative activities and with more generous tax benefits.

The Credit will cover six activities along the innovation value chain (namely research and development done in Singapore; acquisition of intellectual property (IP); registration of IP; investments in design done in Singapore; spending on equipment and software to automate processes; and workers' training).

All businesses will be eligible for the Credit, based on the expenditure they incur in any of the activities. They can deduct 250 per cent of their eligible expenditures on each of these activities from their taxable income, with a cap of SG$300,000 expenditure per activity. This will be effective from Year of Assessment 2011 to Year of Assessment 2015.

Details of the Productivity and Innovation Credit are as follows:

Enhanced Tax Deduction for Research and Development Done in Singapore

To encourage small companies to grow their R&D spending, the Government will give a 250 per cent tax deduction for the first SG$300,000 of qualifying expenses incurred on R&D done in Singapore. The R&D need not necessarily be related to their existing trade.

With this enhancement, the Government will consolidate and phase out the existing R&D tax incentives — namely Research and Development Tax Allowance (RDA)[1] and Research and Development Incentive for Start-up Enterprises (RISE) schemes. No RDA will be granted on chargeable income from Year of Assessment 2011, and RISE will cease with effect from Year of Assessment 2011.

Enhanced Tax Allowance for Intellectual Property Acquisition

The Government will enhance the current 100 per cent tax allowance for IP acquisition by giving an additional 150 per cent tax allowance (i.e. total of 250 per cent) for the first SG$300,000 expenditure on IP acquisition.

Enhanced Tax Deduction for Intellectual Property Registration

To encourage more businesses to register and protect their IP, the Government will extend the existing tax allowance for costs of registering patents to cover the costs of registering other IPs as well, namely trademarks, designs and plant varieties.

It will also increase the quantum of deduction from 100 per cent to 250 per cent for the first SG$300,000 of expenses incurred for registering IP.

Enhanced Tax Deduction for Design Done in Singapore

To encourage more businesses to create new product and industrial designs for the local and international markets, the Government will give businesses a 250 per cent tax deduction for the first SG$300,000 of the qualifying cost incurred for design activities done in Singapore.

This incentive will be administered by DesignSingapore Council.

Enhanced Allowance for Investment in Automation

To encourage businesses to invest in equipment and software that will automate their processes, the Government will grant 250 per cent capital allowance for the first SG$300,000 of expenditure on such investment. It will also update and expand the list of qualifying automation equipment and software to benefit a wider range of sectors.

Enhanced Tax Deduction for Training Costs

To encourage employers to train employees to upgrade their skills, the Government will grant a 250 per cent tax deduction for the first SG$300,000 of expenditure on qualifying workers' training. This enhanced tax deduction can be enjoyed on top of the training support under the WTS and other WDA programmes.

Cash Conversion

To further signal its support for businesses that innovate and improve productivity, the Government will allow businesses the option to convert up to SG$300,000 of their Productivity and Innovation Credit into a non-taxable cash grant of up to SG$21,000.[2] This will support small but growing companies that are investing in technology or upgrading their operations now, but have low taxable income initially. This cash conversion component of the Credit will be available from Year of Assessment 2011 to Year of Assessment 2013, and will be reviewed after three years.

The Productivity and Innovation Credit scheme, inclusive of the cash conversion component, will cost the Government SG$480 million a year.

(C2) National Productivity Fund (New)

The Government will create a National Productivity Fund (NPF) to provide funding for initiatives which are customised to specific industries, clusters and enterprises. The Fund will provide grants to help enterprises in all sectors, with special emphasis initially on sectors where there is potential for larger gains in productivity. The Fund can also serve to develop centres of expertise for a range of industries, which will provide a knowledge base for enterprises to tap on to develop productivity solutions.

The National Productivity and Continuing Education Council will establish the priorities and programmes of the Fund, and tie together the efforts of Singapore's government agencies, industry associations, unions and enterprises.

The Government targets to put SG$2 billion into this new Fund. To begin with, the Government will put SG$1 billion into the Fund in FY2010, which it expects to be able to support initiatives over the next five years.

Construction Sector Initiatives

The Government will dedicate around SG$250 million out of the first SG$1 billion of National Productivity Fund to raising productivity in the construction sector. This will include initiatives to help Singapore's local contractors develop capabilities in areas such as complex civil engineering and building projects, new technologies, and to upgrade to a higher quality workforce.

More details on these construction sector initiatives will be announced during the Ministry of National Development's Committee of Supply.

(D) Raising Foreign Worker Levies

The Government will complement its support for enterprise innovation and upgrading by gradually raising the foreign worker levies, and tightening the levy tiers that are based on the proportion of foreign workers in a company's workforce. The increase in levies will be calibrated and carefully phased in, so as to give companies a clear incentive to upgrade while providing time for them to develop plans to re-gear and grow through productivity improvements. The changes will start with a modest increase in levies in 2010, and will involve further increases over the next two years. The overall dependency ratio for all categories of foreign workers (Work Permit and S Pass holders) will remain unchanged.

As a first step, the Government will raise levy rates for most Work Permit [holders] by between SG$10 and SG$30 on 1 Jul 2010, phasing in further adjustments in levy rates and tiers in 2011 and 2012. Taking the three years together, there will be a total increase of about SG$100 in average levies per worker in manufacturing and services. The construction sector, where there is much scope for productivity improvements, will see a larger increase.

In July 2010, the Government will also sub-divide the current single rate (SG$50) for S Pass workers for all sectors, to two tiers (SG$100 and SG$120). Further adjustments will then be phased in until the rates reach SG$150 and SG$250 by July 2012.

The Ministry of Manpower and Ministry of National Development will release more details of the changes to the Foreign Worker Levy this week.

(E) Supporting Business Restructuring

(E1) Tax Allowance to Defray Acquisition Costs (New)

The Government will introduce, for five years, a one-off tax allowance to help defray a portion of acquisition costs for qualifying Mergers and Acquisitions (M&As).[3] The allowance will have the following features:

- 5 per cent of the value of the qualifying M&A deal;
- The allowance will be capped at SG$5 million;
- The allowance will be written down over five years.

The M&A allowance will be granted to qualifying M&As executed from 1 Apr 2010 to 31 Mar 2015 (both dates inclusive).

(E2) Stamp Duty Relief for Acquisition of Unlisted Shares (New)

The Government will also grant stamp duty relief on the transfer of unlisted shares for qualifying M&A deals. (Currently, listed shares are exempt from stamp duty.) The amount of stamp duty relief will be capped at SG$200,000 per year. This stamp duty relief will be granted to qualifying M&As executed from 1 Apr 2010 to 31 Mar 2015 (both dates inclusive).[4]

The M&A allowance and the stamp duty relief will cost about SG$100 million per year.

(F) Enhancing Land Productivity

(F1) Introduction of Land Intensification Allowance (New)

The Industrial Building Allowance (IBA) was introduced in [the] 1940s to encourage industrialisation. While the

IBA has met its objective, it is no longer adequate or relevant to meet Singapore's current priorities — to promote the intensification of industrial land use towards more land-efficient and higher value-added activities. The Government will phase out IBA, with immediate effect. Existing claimants can continue to claim their remaining IBA until the qualifying expenditures are written down.[5]

The Government will however introduce the Land Intensification Allowance (LIA) for nine sectors identified to have large land-take.[6] The LIA will give businesses in the targeted sectors allowances on the qualifying costs incurred to build qualifying industrial buildings or structures, if they intensify the usage of industrial land to meet or exceed the Gross Plot Ratio (GPR) benchmarks set for each sector. To encourage intensification of industrial lands, the benchmarks will be set around the 75th percentile of the actual GPRs for each sector.

Businesses will be able to claim an initial allowance of 25 per cent and an annual allowance of 5 per cent and can thus fully write down the qualifying costs in 15 years under the LIA — this is more generous than the annual allowance of 3 per cent and full write-down over 25 years under IBA.

The LIA incentive will be in place for five years (with effect from 1 Jul 2010) and will be administered by EDB.

Growing Globally Competitive Companies

(A) Building Capabilities through Partnerships

(A1) Partnerships for Capability Transformation (PACT) (New)

The Local Industry Upgrading Programme (LIUP) has strengthened procurement linkages between MNCs and local companies by building on pre-existing capabilities amongst Singapore suppliers. We will build upon this collaborative approach by focusing on the development of a broader range of new capabilities for our local enterprises, such as helping local enterprises meet stringent manufacturing quality and certification requirements by facilitating their development of requisite competencies. Under the new Partnerships for Capability Transformation (PACT) programme, which will subsume LIUP, the Government will set aside SG$250 million over five years to defray part of the qualifying expenses for such partnerships.

More details will be announced by May 2010.

(A2) Business Associations as Growth Champions (New and Enhanced)

The Government will commit SG$100 million over five years to scale up its support for business associations, including both trade associations and chambers of commerce, to (i) drive productivity at the industry level; (ii) help companies, especially SMEs, build capabilities for growth; and (iii) to facilitate international market access for their members.

More details will be announced by June 2010.

(A3) **Nurturing Future Business Leaders (Enhanced)**

To support the flow of talent to SMEs, the Government will commit SG$45 million over five years to enhance SPRING's Business Leaders Initiative, which is an umbrella programme to attract young talent into SMEs, and groom a future generation of SME managers and entrepreneurs. This includes (i) internship programmes to encourage more polytechnic and university students to choose SMEs as a career of choice; and (ii) support for SMEs to develop talent attraction and retention programmes.

More details will be announced by June 2010.

(B) Reaping Commercial Advantage from R&D

(B1) **National Research Fund Top-up**

The Government will top up the National Research Fund (NRF) with another SG$1.5 billion to support the intensification of our research and development (R&D) efforts.

(B2) **Boost Private Sector R&D**

Private sector R&D spending will be grown from 2 per cent of GDP currently to 2.5 per cent over the next five years. The new Productivity and Innovation Credit scheme, together with the innovation vouchers that SPRING provides to SMEs, and potential partnerships that companies can form with public sector research institutes, will make Singapore one of the most compelling locations for private sector R&D in Asia.

(B3) Catalyse Private Sector R&D through Public-Private Co-Innovation Partnership (New)

The Government will commit SG$450 million over five years to start a Public-Private Co-Innovation Partnership for government agencies to work with private sector companies in co-developing innovative solutions for medium- to long-term needs, in areas such as urban mobility, environmental sustainability and energy security. To give companies greater visibility of the co-innovation opportunities, key government agencies will share their technology roadmaps and future needs publicly. As part of the co-innovation process, grants will be provided to help companies build R&D capabilities and test-bed innovative solutions.

More details will be announced by July 2010.

(C) Improving Access to Growth Finance

(C1) Tax Deduction for Angel Investors Scheme (New)

An eligible angel investor who commits a minimum of SG$100,000 of equity investment in a qualifying start-up in a Year of Assessment (YA) can claim a tax deduction at 50 per cent of his investment quantum, at the end of a two-year holding period. The deduction is capped at SG$500,000 of investments into qualifying start-ups per YA.

SPRING will announce the details by June 2010. However, the incentive will apply to qualifying investments made from 1 Mar 2010 to 31 Mar 2015.

(C2) Catalyse Growth Capital through Co-Investment (New)

The Government will catalyse financing for companies that have achieved initial success and are looking to scale up. To provide a significant boost, the Government will mobilise up to SG$1.5 billion of growth capital by seeding a range of funds over 10 years, for which the Government will contribute up to half the capital. The programme will be implemented in phases, and will grow in tandem with the appetite of the investing community and with the number of companies they find attractive. The first phase will be launched this year, with the Government providing up to SG$250 million to match private sector investments. This will allow for a few funds to be established, with a total of SG$500 million of growth capital for Singapore-based enterprises.

More details would be announced by May 2010.

(C3) Government's Role in Cross-Border Financing (Under study)

The Government is studying various models and evaluating how best we can realise the development of a market-based institution to support and catalyse the growth of cross-border financing for Singapore-based companies. Such an institution must be commercially-managed, with the discipline to generate a fair return commensurate with the risks. Its business model must also involve collaboration with other financial institutions.

(D) Growing Our Role as a Global Business Hub

(D1) Development and Expansion Incentive Scheme (Extended)

The Development and Expansion Incentive (DEI) scheme will be extended to law practices registered in Singapore as a company or as a branch of a foreign company providing international legal services so as to enhance our position as an arbitration hub. Under this incentive, approved law practices will enjoy a 10 per cent concessionary tax rate on incremental income derived from performing international legal services. This incentive is valid from 1 Apr 2010 to 31 Mar 2015.

More details will be announced by [the] Ministry of Law and EDB by March 2010.

(D2) Promote Financial Services (Enhanced)

The Government will continue to update tax incentives to ensure that they remain relevant and encourage institutions to build up high-value activities and expand the number of professional jobs in Singapore. Salient changes will be:

a. Simplification of the taxation rules and updating of the list of incentivised activities for the Financial Sector Incentive;
b. Streamlining of the tax incentives for futures members of Singapore Exchange (SGX) and members of Singapore Commodity Exchange Ltd (SICOM); and

c.   Renewal of the income tax, stamp duty and GST
     concessions for listed real estate investment trusts
     and renewal of GST concessions for qualifying listed
     registered business trusts for the period from 18 Feb
     2010 to 31 Mar 2015.

(D3) Boost Transportation Hub (New and Enhanced)

To further develop Singapore as an International Maritime
Centre, the Government will:

a.   Introduce a five-year tax incentive from 1 Apr 2010
     to 31 Mar 2015 which grants a concessionary tax rate
     of 10 per cent for ship brokers and forward freight
     agreement traders;
b.   Renew the Maritime Finance Incentive upon its expiry
     on 28 Feb 2011 for another five years to 31 Mar 2016;
     and
c.   Expand the scope of GST zero-rating for the marine
     industry, by expanding the definition of qualifying
     ships and extending GST zero-rating to goods and
     services provided to qualifying ships, with effect from
     1 Jul 2010.

To further enhance our competitiveness in the Maintenance, Repair and Overhaul industry, the Government will
renew the Investment Allowance scheme which grants an
additional 50 per cent allowance (on top of normal capital
allowance) for aircraft rotables for another five years from
1 Apr 2010 to 31 Mar 2015. The rules for claiming the
allowance will also be liberalised.

(D4) Reduce GST Compliance Costs (New and Enhanced)

The Government will introduce several GST-related changes to ease compliance costs for businesses:

a. To ease import GST cash flow for importers, a new scheme will be introduced to allow approved businesses to import goods without upfront payment of GST when the goods enter Singapore. Under the scheme, approved businesses will be allowed to defer their import GST payments for at least a month. The scheme will take effect from 1 Oct 2010; and

b. Simplify the rules for the accounting of GST to the earlier of the date of payment or the date of invoice. This will reduce administrative costs for most businesses, particularly smaller traders, as they no longer need to track the date of delivery of goods or performance of services. The changes will take effect from 1 Jan 2011.

(E) Other Tax Measures

(E1) Enhanced Transport Technology Innovation Development Scheme (TIDES+) (Enhanced)

To support the development and test-bedding of transport technologies, green vehicles brought to Singapore for the purpose of test-bedding can enjoy waiver of Additional Registration Fees, Certificate of Entitlement, and custom duties for an initial period of six years, up from the existing two years. In addition, the quota of vehicles under this scheme will expanded from 300 vehicles up to 1,300. The total amount of tax waived is estimated to be about SG\$75 million.

(E2) Green Vehicle Rebate (Extended)

Currently, only owners of brand new green vehicles are entitled to the Green Vehicle Rebate. To encourage the greater use of low-carbon transportation, the scope of the Green Vehicle Rebate scheme will be extended to include imported used green vehicles with effect from 1 Jul 2010.

(E3) Withholding Tax for Public Entertainers (Enhanced)

The Government will reduce the withholding tax rate for non-resident public entertainers from 15 per cent to 10 per cent on their gross income derived in respect of services performed in Singapore. This reduction will help local organisers to attract more internationally-rated acts and performances to Singapore. The 10 per cent tax rate will take effect from Budget Day (i.e. 22 Feb 2010) and will end on 31 Mar 2015.

(E4) Duty-Free Liquor Allowance (Enhanced)

The Government will allow travellers to purchase an additional litre of duty-free wine or beer in lieu of one litre of duty-free spirits. Travellers who prefer wine or beer to spirits can therefore enjoy duty-free allowance on two litres of wine and one litre of beer, or one litre of wine and two litres of beer. This change will take effect from 1 Apr 2010.

Benefits for Households

Including All Singaporeans in Growth

The Government will be spending SG$1.4 billion in direct transfers for households in FY2010. Inclusive of the Workfare Income Supplement, the total sum transferred to households is SG$1.8 billion.

(A) Shift to a Progressive Property Tax Regime

(A1) Shifting to a Progressive Property Tax Regime (New)

Currently, owner-occupied residential properties are taxed at a concessionary 4 per cent rate (instead of 10 per cent for all other properties). In addition, owner-occupied residential properties with Annual Values (AVs) below SG$10,000 can enjoy the on-going 1994 property tax rebates ranging from SG$25 to SG$150, depending on the AVs of their properties.

For property tax payable from January 2011, the existing 1994 property tax rebates will be replaced by a progressive property tax schedule for owner-occupied residential properties. Three tiers of property tax rates for such properties will be introduced — 0 per cent, 4 per cent and 6 per cent:

- 0 per cent for the first SG$6,000 of AV;
- 4 per cent for the next SG$59,000 of AV;
- 6 per cent for the balance of AV in excess of SG$65,000.

The new property tax system will benefit most Singaporeans. All owner-occupied homes will enjoy tax savings of SG$240 as a result of the exemption of the first SG$6,000 of AV. This will mean that all HDB flat owners and the large majority of private property owners will pay lower taxes.

Owners of high-end properties with AVs of more than SG$77,000, will see a small increase in tax payable, as their effective tax rates will be higher than the current 4 per cent. They comprise the top 3 per cent of private owner-occupied residential properties, or the top 0.4 per cent of all owner-occupied homes in Singapore.

Non-owner-occupied residential properties and other properties will continue to be subject to 10 per cent property tax.

(B) Increasing Tax Reliefs for Families

(B1) Enhancing Parent Relief (Enhanced)

A taxpayer may claim this relief if he supported his or his spouse's parents, grandparents and great-[grand]parents in the previous year.

To provide greater recognition for those who are looking after parents, grandparents and great-[grand] parents, the parent relief will be increased to:

a. SG$7,000 (from SG$5,000 currently) for taxpayers who are staying with their dependants;
b. SG$4,500 (from SG$3,500 currently) for taxpayers who are not staying with their dependants;

c. SG$11,000 (from SG$8,000 currently) for taxpayers who are staying with their handicapped dependants; and

d. SG$8,000 (from SG$6,500 currently) for taxpayers who are not staying with their handicapped dependants.

These changes will be implemented from Year of Assessment 2010.

(B2) Enhancing Wife Relief to Spouse Relief (Enhanced)

With effect from Year of Assessment 2010, the Government will allow wives who are taxpayers to claim a spouse relief of SG$2,000, similar to the current scheme for husbands. This will help families where the wife is the breadwinner, for instance where the husband has retired. Accordingly, wife relief will be renamed as "spouse relief."

(B3) Raising of Income Threshold of Dependants for Taxpayers to Claim Dependant-Related Reliefs (Enhanced)

Currently, the income of the dependant cannot exceed SG$2,000 in the preceding year if a taxpayer wishes to claim the following dependant-related reliefs:

- Handicapped Sibling Relief;
- Wife Relief;
- Handicapped Spouse Relief;
- Parent Relief;
- Handicapped Parent Relief;
- Qualifying Child Relief;
- Handicapped Child Relief;
- Working Mother's Child Relief;

- CPF Cash Top-up Relief for top-ups into the CPF accounts of spouses or siblings.

The Government will increase the income threshold for dependant-related reliefs from SG$2,000 to SG$4,000.

In recognition of the extra resources and attention needed in providing care for the disabled, the Government will also remove the income threshold for handicapped dependant-related relief.

The changes for the dependant-related reliefs will be implemented from Year of Assessment 2010, except for the CPF Cash Top-up Relief for top-ups to the CPF accounts of spouse and siblings (for which the changes to the income threshold will be effective from Year of Assessment 2011).

(C) Increase Course Fee Relief

(C1) Increasing Course Fee Relief (Enhanced)

To support for lifelong learning, the Government will increase the course fees relief from SG$3,500 to SG$5,500 with effect from Year of Assessment 2011.

(D) Support for Charitable Giving

(D1) Extending Tax Deduction for Donations (Extended)

In Budget 2009, the Government had increased the tax deduction for donations made in 2009 to Institutions of Public Character (IPCs) and other approved institutions from 200 per cent to 250 per cent.

The Government will extend this measure for an additional year, to give additional support to charitable giving as the economy recovers.

(E) Measures to Support Households

(E1) Top-up to Central Provident Fund-Medisave Accounts (CPF-MA) (Enhanced)

The Government will provide a one-off top-up to the CPF-Medisave Accounts of older Singaporeans. Details are given in the table below.

Annual Assessable Income (AI) in 2009	Annual Value of Home in 2009	
	Up to SG$6,000	*More than SG$6,000*
Up to SG$29,000[7]	Aged[8] 50–59: **SG$300**	Aged 50–59: **SG$200**
	Aged 60–69: **SG$400**	Aged 60–69: **SG$300**
	Aged 70 and above: **SG$500**	Aged 70 and above: **SG$400**
SG$29,001–SG$100,000		
More than SG$100,000	SG$0	

(E2) Top-ups to Medifund and ElderCare Endowment Fund (Enhanced)

As part of its ongoing efforts to set aside funds to meet Singaporeans' long term healthcare needs, the Government will set aside in Budget 2010 SG$200 million each for the following Funds:

a. **Medifund**, which supports needy Singaporeans;
b. **ElderCare Fund**, which supports the needs of elderly Singaporeans with their long-term healthcare needs.

(E3) Top-up to Post-Secondary Education Account (Enhanced)

The Government will provide a top-up of SG$230 million to the Post-Secondary Education Account (PSEA) accounts of young Singaporeans.

Details of the top-up are given in the table below.

	Annual Value of Home in 2009	
Age in 2010	Up to SG$11,000	More than SG$ 11,000
7 to 12	SG$200	SG$100
13 to 20	SG$500	SG$250

(F) Raising Productivity

(F1) Introduction of Workfare Training Scheme (WTS) (New)

The Government will introduce a three-year Workfare Training Scheme (WTS) to complement the Workfare Income Supplement (WIS) scheme. The WTS will:

* Subsidise 90 per cent to 95 per cent of absentee payroll and course fee outlay for employers, when they send their older low-wage workers for training;
* Provide cash grants, capped at SG$400 per year, when WIS recipients complete their training;

- Introduce a structured training programme for those with very low skills, including those who are unemployed.

(F2) Enhancement of Workfare Income Supplement (Enhanced)

The Government will enhance the Workfare Income Supplement (WIS) as follows:

- *Higher payouts.* Maximum payouts for the WIS will be increased by between SG$150 and SG$400, with more going to older workers to encourage them to remain in the workforce;
- *Extension to more workers.* Those earning up to SG$1,700 per month will now be eligible for WIS, up from the current limit of SG$1,500 per month.

Further details of the enhancements to Workfare (WIS and WTS) will be announced during the Ministry of Manpower's Committee of Supply.

Notes

1. For taxpayers with unutilised RDA granted for Year of Assessment 2009 and Year of Assessment 2010, they may opt to utilise the RDA as further deductions against their incremental R&D expenses from Year of Assessment 2011 until Year of Assessment 2016, as under the RDA scheme currently. Alternatively, they can elect instead to claim the 250 per cent tax deduction for the first SG$300,000 of their qualifying R&D expenses incurred for Year of Assessment 2011 to Year of Assessment 2015.
2. Up to SG$300,000 of tax deductions and allowances arising from expenditure on the six activities covered under the Productivity

and Innovation Credit can be converted into [a] cash grant at a conversion rate of 7 per cent. 7 per cent is higher than the median effective tax rate of taxpaying companies including SMEs, for which the enhanced tax benefits under the Credit aim to especially benefit.

3. Previously, interest expenses incurred in acquisitions could be deducted against taxable dividend income under the imputation system. This is no longer possible under our 1-tier system as dividends are not taxed. The new M&A allowance is designed for simplicity. It also does not distinguish between interest costs and other costs. In particular, it is neutral between debt and equity in financing qualifying M&A transactions.

4. IRAS will release more details of the M&A allowance and stamp duty relief scheme by June 2010. The full stamp duty on such transfers of unlisted shares will continue to be payable on all transfers of unlisted shares until details of the scheme including the definition of qualifying M&A deals are finalised. IRAS will subsequently refund the stamp duty paid if a deal, which is executed on and after 1 Apr 2010 but before the finalisation of the rules, can satisfy the finalised rules.

5. Qualifying capital expenditures incurred by businesses on or before 22 Feb 2010 on the construction or purchase of qualifying industrial buildings will continue to qualify for IBA, subject to existing IBA rules.

6. The nine sectors are: pharmaceuticals, petroleum, other chemicals, aerospace, solar cell manufacturing, petrochemicals, specialties, semiconductor-wafer fabrication as well as marine and offshore engineering.

7. Based on the median gross annual income of employed residents (i.e. full-time and part-time) in 2008. The income threshold will also be adjusted for 2010 GST Credits and Senior Citizens' Bonus.

8. Age in 2010

References

ASEAN Studies Centre. *Global Financial Crisis: Implications for ASEAN*. Singapore: Institute of Southeast Asian Studies, 2009.

Asian Development Bank (ADB). *The Global Economic Crisis: Challenges for Developing Asia and ADB's Response*. Manila: ADB, February 2009.

Bhaskaran, Manu, ed. *The Eleventh Singapore Economic Roundtable*. Singapore: Straits Times Press Reference, June 2009.

Bhaskaran, Manu. "How Will the Global Economy Affect Asia in 2010?" *The Edge Singapore*, December 2009.

Bhaskaran, Manu. "Reassessing Singapore's Economic Future". *The Edge Singapore*, July 2009.

Chibber, Ajay, Jayati Ghosh, and Thangavel Palanivel. *The Global Financial Crisis and the Asia-Pacific Region, A Synthesis Study Incorporating Evidence from Country Case Studies*. New York: UNDP, November 2009.

Chow, Penn Nee, Ho Woei Chin, and Jimmy Koh. "Singapore Budget 2009: An Unprecedented Budget for Unprecedented Times", 22 January 2009 <http://www.uobgroup.com/assets/pdfs/research/CA-SIN_22Jan09.pdf>.

Citigroup Global Markets Report. *Asia Macro View: Ten Asia Themes for the New Decade*, 2 February 2010.

DBS Group Research. "Economics Markets Strategy 1Q 2010", 10 December 2009 <https://www.dbsvresearch.com/research/DBS/research.nsf/(vwAllDocs)/5E7ADFECC782D0F8482576880030033C/$FILE/dbs_qtrly_091210.pdf>.

DBS Group Research. "Economics Markets Strategy 4Q 2009", 17 September 2009 <https://www.dbsvresearch.com/research/DBS/research.nsf/(vwAllDocs)/C1888A331CECB1B648257634003B66D5/$FILE/dbs_qtrly_090917.pdf>.

Department of Statistics, Singapore. *Yearbook of Statistics Singapore* (various years). Singapore: Department of Statistics.

Economic Development Board (EDB) Singapore. *Report on the Census for Industrial Production* (various years). Singapore: EDB.

Economist Intelligence Unit. *Country Reports* (various issues).

Eskesen, Leif Lybecker. *The Role for Counter-Cyclical Fiscal Policy in Singapore*. International Monetary Fund Working Paper, January 2009.

Government of Singapore. *Report of the Economic Strategies Committee: High Skilled People, Innovative Economy, Distinctive Global City*. Singapore: Government of Singapore, February 2010.

Hussain, Zakir. "Paradigm Shift or Pendulum Swing? *Straits Times*, 6 February 2010.

International Monetary Fund (IMF). *Global Financial Stability Report: Financial Market Turbulence — Causes, Consequences and Policies*. Washington, DC: IMF, October 2007.

――――. *World Economic Outlook April 2009: Crisis and Recovery*. Washington, DC: IMF, April 2009.

――――. *Global Financial Stability Report: Navigating the Financial Challenges Ahead*. Washington, DC: IMF, October 2009.

――――. *World Economic Outlook October 2009: Sustaining the Recovery*. Washington, DC: IMF, October 2009.

――――. *World Economic Outlook Update: A Policy-driven Multispeed Recovery*. Washington, DC: IMF, 26 January 2010.

Jang-Sup, Shin and Daniel Soh. *Impact of a Global Recession on a Small Open Economy* <www.SERIWorld.org>.

Keat, Heng Swee. "The Global Financial Crisis – Impact on Asia and Policy Challenges Ahead". Paper presented at Federal Reserve Bank of San Francisco, Asia Economic Policy Conference: Asia and the Global Financial Crisis, 18–20 October 2009.

――――. *The Impact of the Global Financial Crisis on Asia*. Keynote speech at the International Institute of Finance (IIF) Asia Regional Economic Forum, Singapore, 4 March 2009.

Ketels, Christian, Ashish Lall, and Neo Boon Siong. *Singapore Competitiveness Report 2009*. Singapore: Asia Competitiveness

Institute, Lee Kuan Yew School of Public Policy, National University of Singapore.

Ministry of Finance (MOF), Singapore. *Budget Highlight Financial Year 2009*. Singapore: MOF, January 2009.

_____. *Budget Highlight Financial Year 2010*. Singapore: MOF, February 2010.

Ministry of Trade and Industry, Singapore. *Economic Survey of Singapore* (various annual and quarterly issues). Singapore: Ministry of Trade and Industry.

Mohan, Rakesh. *Global Financial Crisis: Causes, Impact, Policy Responses and Lessons*. 7th Annual India Business Forum Conference, London Business School, 23 April 2009.

Monetary Authority of Singapore (MAS). *Singapore's Exchange Rate Policy*. Singapore: MAS, February 2001.

_____ *Financial Stability Review*. Singapore: MAS, November 2008.

_____. *Macroeconomic Review* 8, no. 1 (April 2009).

_____. *Macroeconomic Review* 8, no. 2 (October 2009).

_____. *Financial Stability Review*. Singapore: MAS, November 2009.

_____. "News Archive — Parliamentary Replies". <http://www.mas.gov.sg/news_room/parliamentary_questions/parliamentary_questions_index.html>.

Nigam Kee Jin. "Coping with the Asian Financial Crisis: The Singapore Experience." ISEAS Visiting Researchers Series No. 8. Singapore: Institute of Southeast Asian Studies, March 2000.

Tan, Augustine H.H. "The Asian Economic Crisis: The Way Ahead for Singapore" <www.fas.nus.edu.sg> May 1999.

Thangavelu, Shandre M. *Global Financial Crisis: Impact on Singapore and ASEAN*. EABER Working Paper Series no. 49, 29 November 2008 (preliminary draft).

Truman, Edwin M. *The Global Financial Crisis: Lessons Learned and Challenges for Developing Countries*. Washington, DC: Peterson Institute for International Economics.

UNCTAD. *The Global Economic Crisis: Systemic Failures and Multilateral Remedies*. New York: United Nations, April, 2009.

Index

About the Author

Sanchita Basu Das is the Lead Researcher for Economic Affairs in the ASEAN Studies Centre at the Institute of Southeast Asian Studies, Singapore. Prior to that, she worked in the private sector as an economist at Consulting Engineering Services, India, ABN AMRO Bank, India and United Overseas Bank, Singapore. She has published her research widely and has also edited two special issues of the journal, *ASEAN Economic Bulletin*. She writes book chapters and articles with regular frequency, on economic and financial issues facing Southeast Asia and ASEAN regionalism among other topics. She has an MBA from the National University of Singapore and an MA from the Delhi School of Economics (India).

www.ingramcontent.com/pod-product-compliance
Lightning Source LLC
Chambersburg PA
CBHW021813270326
41932CB00007B/170